BULLETPROOF FLOWERS FOR THE SOUTH

Bulletproof Flowers for the South

JIM WILSON

TAYLOR PUBLISHING COMPANY
DALLAS, TEXAS

*To my Mississippi-born mother, Inez Penley Wilson,
southern to the bone, who loved children and flowers.*

Designed by David Timmons

Published by Taylor Publishing Company
1550 West Mockingbird Lane
Dallas, Texas 75235
www.taylorpub.com

Library of Congress Cataloging-in-Publication Data:

Wilson, James W. (James Wesley), 1925–
    Bulletproof flowers for the South / by Jim Wilson.
        p.   cm.
    Includes index.
ISBN 0-87833-245-6
    1. Flower gardening—Southern States. 2. Flowers—Southern States I. Title
SB406.65.S85W56   1999
635.69'0975—dc21   99-16703
                                                       CIP

10 9 8 7 6 5 4 3 2 1
Printed in the United States of America

Page i, Willow-leafed perennial sunflower (*Helianthus salicifolius*). Page iii, Confederate rose (*Hibiscus mutabilis*) Belton Middle School wildflower meadow, Belton, SC. Page iv, Joseph's coat (*Amaranthus tricolor*) at "Rosalie" estate, Natchez, Mississippi. Page vi, Two varieties of garden sage (*Salvia officinalis*): foreground, 'Bergartten'; background, common or narrow-leafed.

Contents

Introduction

You don't have to have been born in the South to understand what I am about to tell you. All you have to do is garden through one season of our summer heat and humidity, and it will become clear as a bell. *Our special climates demand special flowers—bulletproof flowers.* Just one season's experience, and anyone can understand why only certain kinds of flowers can flourish in our trying climates. You'll see the need for flowers that, after planting in the spring, will stay in color right through the summer, perhaps until the first fall frost. No experienced southern gardener wants to prepare soil for replanting during weather so hot and sticky that you can't lift a hand without breaking into a sweat. So we value flowers that will keep on keeping on. Let the botanical gardens and theme parks swap out their flowers four or five times during the year, bless their sweaty little hearts.

We need flowers and foliage plants that are in for the long haul.

Bulletproof Flowers

If you're wondering where the term "bulletproof flowers" came from, I heard it first from the producer of *The Victory Garden*, Russell Morash of WGBH-TV. Russell used it to describe flowers and foliage plants that will stay in color through most of the summer despite prolonged high heat and humidity. The best of these, when spring planted, will provide continuous color until fall frost. Others may provide color in waves, with periods of green foliage in between. Still others may look shabby during the dog days, but will recover and bloom again with the coming of cool weather. This book also includes some hardy perennials and herbs which may stay in color for a month or two, but will also provide good form, texture, and shades of green or gray for the remainder of the growing season. Some bulletproof flowers are tropicals which, except in the Deep South,

Southeastern wildflowers at the Wilson home

either have to be grown as annuals and sacrificed at the end of the growing season, carried indoors through the winter, or saved as rooted cuttings taken from tip growth or from saved rhizomes.

Eight States and Parts of Six More

Just what do I include in "the South"? For purposes of definition, I included all the states from Virginia west through southeastern Kansas, eastern Oklahoma, and East Texas. I included lowland parts of Kentucky and the southern edge of Missouri, except the high Ozarks. I stopped where the tall timber in eastern Oklahoma and East Texas begins to grade into the Great Plains or dryland country. I included everything south of Virginia except from central Florida on down. They can grow so many semi-tropical and tropical kinds down there that the information in this book wouldn't help them much.

For years, I defined "the South" as any place where bermudagrass thrives, but I'm beginning to see patches of it far north of where you'd normally expect to find it. I would suggest kudzu as a southern indicator plant were it not for my having seen a hillside covered with kudzu in Bronx, New York!

Advantages of Growing Bulletproof Flowers

What advantages do bulletproof flowers offer to southern gardeners who have to cope with uncomfortable heat and humidity several months of the year? You can plant early in the season and spread mulch to keep weeds from overwhelming your flowers. Then, except for a few weed-pulling forays during early morning or late evening hours, and watering during dry spells, you can sit on your screened porch, drink sweet tea, and enjoy color throughout the summer. What a change from bygone days when the South saw a long, mostly green hiatus from the end of azalea bloom season to the beginning of camellia bloom time. Now you can luxuriate in color all summer long!

The Only Constant Is Change

For the past several years I've lectured on gardening from Richmond, Virginia, to Tulsa, Oklahoma, and from Orlando to the American Queen paddlewheeler down the lower Mississippi. I've visited scores of private gardens and garden centers in the South, and I'm convinced that virtually everything about flower gardening in the South is changing rapidly, and for the better. Soil preparation and garden maintenance have been improved and simplified, but the major change is in the flowers and foliage plants we are using in landscapes and outdoor containers.

I can remember when most gardeners in the South grew flowers from direct-seeding, or from seedlings started on a windowsill and later moved to a coldframe. Prior to World War II, most of the plants sold in seed stores (there were no garden centers as we know them now) were vegetables: tomatoes, peppers, sweet potatoes, onions, and cabbage. Oh, a few blooming pansy plants might be displayed in the fall, sold in bunches, but there were no big spring displays of bedding plants already showing color. A few greenhouses on the outskirts of major cities sold

Iguana pot from Guadalajara, Mexico, with the heat-resistant pentas 'Cranberry Punch' and 'Pearl'

Ornamental pepper plants being set out by wax-leafed begonias

started plants of flowers, but they were marketed prior to bloom stage, and were sliced out of sheetcakes of composted soil a dozen at a time, from wooden flats. The age of plastics was still in the future.

Mass production of bedding plants began during the 1950s. Plant breeders began concentrating on developing short plants that would bloom quickly after seeding in pots. Market packs and plugs soon replaced individual small pots. And breeders began to pay attention to the gradual shifting of demand from sun-loving kinds to shade-tolerant plants. Zinnias, marigolds, and petunias were bumped out of their top places in gardens by impatiens, wax-leafed begonias, and (in the South) periwinkle. Not until recent years, however, did seed breeders acknowledge the special needs of southern gardens in their plant improvement programs.

Winter weeds work against growing hardy perennials in the South. Were it not for the increasing use of mulches to keep down weeds, we wouldn't be as far along with perennials as we are today. We were accustomed to turning the soil after cleaning off spent annuals, and turning it again before spring planting, to reduce the weed population and to incorporate limestone and fertilizer. Mulching makes turning the soil unnecessary, but frequent liming of gardens is still needed, even on azaleas, rhododendrons, and blueberries growing on our degraded soils. University of Georgia trials and landscape experience by nurserymen indicate that many so-called "acid-loving" plants can benefit from liming with dolomitic limestone to correct calcium and magnesium deficiencies that are, in some parts of the South, profound.

Tropical and Semi-Tropical Plants in the Middle and Upper South

Perhaps the most important contributor to the change in southern gardens is the surge of interest in semi-tropical and tropical plants in the United States Department of Agriculture (USDA) hardiness zones six, seven, and eight. Most of the species had reached Florida years earlier by way of the Caribbean Islands, Mexico, or Central America, and some had entered California from South Africa,

Australia, New Zealand, and southeast Asia. Home gardeners and professional growers fell in love with these exotic species when on winter vacations, brought plants home, and discovered that most grew very well during the summers in the Middle and Upper South. They then had to convince local growers to produce plants or order them from growers in Florida or along the Gulf Coast, or from California. You might call the process "pulling plants through the supply channel." Now, producers and marketers are "pushing them through," to capitalize on the appeal of new and different flowers.

Award-Winning Flowers

Recently, we have begun to see plant introductions developed primarily for growing in containers or hanging baskets, and secondarily for ground beds. Evaluation and promotional organizations such as Proven Winners and FloraStar are behind the introduction of these cutting-grown or micropropagated cultivars. Many of these new flowers were originally from hot countries, but not all of them are tolerant of high humidity.

A much more venerable organization, All-America Selections (est. 1932), specializes in evaluating flowers and vegetables that are

Star cluster flower (*Pentas lanceolata*) with garden statuary, Baton Rouge, Louisiana

customarily grown from seeds. To be entered in their trials, a flower should be an annual or a precocious perennial that will bloom the first year from seeds. A new introduction that is proven in field trials to be significantly better than the reigning "best in its class" will be given an All-America Selections award. Winners include both cool-weather and warm-weather kinds, so you have to rely on seed catalog and seed packet descriptions to lead you to ones that will stand up under heat and humidity.

Perennials, too, have organizations for evaluating the potential of relatively recent introductions. Foremost is the Perennial Plant Association, which evaluates hardy cultivars and each year announces the Perennial Plant of the Year. Although their test grounds are weighted to the north, most of their winners will also grow well through hardiness zone eight. Certain of the hardy perennials have difficulty adjusting to our hot summer nights. Dr. Marc Cathey's new American Horticultural Society Plant Heat-Zone Map addresses the problem, and assigning internationally recognized numerical heat tolerance ratings to perennial cultivars is well under way.

This revolution in southern flower gardening is far from over, and bulletproof flowers are one of the most visible results. Water gardens are appearing in more landscapes, as well as multipurpose trees, shrubs, and vines that offer not only shade but also colorful blossoms, fall color, and winter berries. Altogether, they have reclaimed the summer months for garden enjoyment. No longer is there a long, all-green summer hiatus. We can have loads of color twelve months of the year in the South, and it is surprisingly simple to do.

Black-eyed Susan (*Rudbeckia fulgida*) with crested celosia at the Park Seed Co. trials

ONE

What's So Special about Southern Gardens and Southern Gardeners?

It's a shame that we southern gardeners have to put up with misconceptions about the South fostered by "Bubba" jokes and fallout from books about trashy people. Most of us just smile and consider the source. We know that Bubba is too busy tinkering with his pickup truck or Harley to plant more than a turnip patch, and that trashy people can be found in every state in the Union. Besides, we prefer to have no truck with people who don't appreciate the better things of life, especially gardening.

This book doesn't deny that much of the South has to suffer through prolonged high heat and an uncomfortable level of humidity for several months of the year. (Hisses and boos from the Chambers of Commerce in the South!) The further south you travel, the worse it gets. We southern gardeners don't fight it, however; we just schedule our garden tasks for early in the morning or late in the evening, and we try to complete major landscaping jobs during the cool months of the year. Prolonged high heat and humidity aren't all bad. They make it possible to grow many kinds of plants that folks up north can't. And our mild winters can produce minor horticultural miracles by turning some plants normally considered annuals into perennials.

A Long Tradition of Gardening

Tradition holds that a Charleston, South Carolina, planter, a few years after Charleston's founding in the 1600s, made the first use of a landscape architect in designing a garden in the colonies. Yet, evidence exists of formal gardens in southern Louisiana at about the same date. They also may have been laid out by gardeners or landscape artists brought over from Europe. The Creole influence still shows in many old plantation gardens along the lower Mississippi River.

One shouldn't become so dazzled by these great gardens of the top 2 or 3 percent of the southern population of those days that they overlook what was going on with the much larger part. During the expansion of the southern colonies from their toehold along the Atlantic, a few town gardens were bedecked with flowers, but out on the frontier and around slave quarters, vegetable and herb gardens far outnumbered the few flower beds. Those flower beds included bulbs of durable kinds and varieties of flowers that set copious crops of seeds. Plantation gardens, on the other hand, included some species from Caribbean islands such as Barbados and Martinique, from where many British and French planters moved with their slaves during the late seventeenth and early eighteenth centuries. There were even a few kinds ordered from Europe or brought over by skilled gardeners moving to the new land.

Reconstruction or Destruction?

The South suffered longer than most people realize after the War Between the States, during the period called "Reconstruction." During Reconstruction, the slow recovery was partly the doings of northern commercial interests who were determined to maintain a competitive edge over southern manufacturers. A lingering nostalgia for "the old ways" and the "lost cause" of the South also impeded change. During the War and for several succeeding decades, the competitive advantage enjoyed by the North allowed huge industrial empires to be built, and a strong, upwardly-mobile middle class developed. The point of this look back is to show how it happened that the North surged ahead of the South, which had once led in horticultural sophistication. The new industrial barons visited Europe and brought back skilled gardeners, new plants, and ideas for greenhouses and conservatories. Some of their homes and grounds were converted to botanical or estate gardens upon the death of wealthy owners, while many of the finest southern plantations were abandoned. To this day, for example, much more is known about hardy perennials and houseplants in the North than below the Mason-Dixon line. For nearly a century, gardeners in the South had virtually no botanical gardens where they could observe plants and learn how to grow them.

Many of the surviving plantations had passed into the hands of wealthy northerners, and there was little money or means for the average southerner to travel or to experiment with new and different kinds of plants. The merchant class in the South was slow to become affluent because their customers were poor. With the exception of the birth of garden clubs in Georgia during the 1920s, horticultural progress stalled until about the time of World War II.

Roots in the Country

Until World War II days, you would seldom find a southern family so urbanized that they had no relatives out in the country. The link between country and city people and gardens was still strong, and most families cultivated sizable food gardens. They didn't have to study gardening; they absorbed it from the older, farm-reared generation. They grew a lot of annual flowers, either from saved seeds or from seed packets purchased from displays in general stores. Bulbs, rhizomes, tubers, and corms were passed along from generation to generation. Common names proliferated. At that time, hardy perennials were little known in the South, except by specialists such as the legendary Elizabeth Lawrence of North Carolina. Much more was known about such southern specialties as camellias, azaleas, semi-hardy summer bulbs, Louisiana iris, and southern cultivars of roses.

Critter Consciousness

We southern gardeners are more aware of the critters around us than are gardeners in the North, and with good reason. Gardeners most everywhere have to be careful about poison ivy, ticks, mosquitoes, deer flies, and venomous reptiles and arachnids, but chiggers and no-see-ums are mostly a southern problem, and imported fire ants have been reported as far north as Maryland. We are afflicted with squirrels, rabbits, and deer, just like northern gardeners, but gardeners in the Deep South have to contend with armadillos as well. On the other hand, woodchucks don't range much past the Upper South. I know it is hard to accept critter damage gracefully, but then I think of Europe, where fully half of their native animal and plant species have been exterminated, and to a point, I am willing to make allowances.

The New Melting Pot

Five decades ago, southern communities that had been virtually isolated since their founding began seeing families move in from other parts of North America and the rest of the world. The newcomers brought with them new preferences in landscape designs, flowers, and herbs, and sometimes a pervasive lack of information on how to garden in tune with our seasons, heat, and humidity.

Scholars of African-American cultures have begun studying the unique gardening and landscaping habits handed down from Africa by researching the few remaining homes and landscapes from two or three hundred years ago along the east coast of Africa (see Appendix). There is no doubt that many kinds of vegetables and flowers were brought to this country by slaves, sometimes following generations of servitude on Caribbean plantations, and we owe much of the richness of southern cooking and southern landscapes to their introductions.

This rich mixture of ethnic groups and economic classes has set the stage for a transformation in southern gardens and plants. I've been watching it for more than fifty years of gardening as an adult, through the post–*Victory Garden* days, through the flower-children era, and through the expansion of suburbs. Yet, this is the first time I've felt like fastening my seat belt.

Cotton Clothes and Skin-So-Soft

Our summer days are shorter than those in states further north but our sun really bears down. Veteran gardeners in the South suit up before going out for chores. Shorts and short-sleeved shirts are risky because of the likelihood of sunburn and skin cancer, and broad-brimmed straw hats and sunblock lotion are in. Many of us choose garden clothing that fits loosely and is made of pure cotton for improved absorption. During mosquito season we rub on Avon Skin-So-Soft bath oil; it does the trick. Whether it is the floral scent or the oils in it that repel mosquitoes, the manufacturer isn't disclosing.

❧ TWO ☙

Must I Learn Everything about Gardening All Over Again?

What hit me?" a gardener might ask when faced with our summer heat and humidity. Or perhaps he or she arrived during our mild fall or winter season and became lulled into believing that there was still plenty of time to study up on southern gardening. But let's say that we had one of those years when summer comes sizzling in on the heels of winter, canceling our usual delightful spring season. After struggling with heat and humidity for a few weeks, the stunned transplant from cooler climates is more likely to ask, "Where did I go wrong?"

Where *Did* I Go Wrong?

Again and again I've seen northern gardeners newly arrived in the South, demoralized by the prospect of relearning everything they knew about gardening. The further north their former home, the greater the feeling of dislocation and confusion, and it happens to experienced gardeners as well as to novices. All of a sudden, they have from seven to eleven months of frost-free weather in which to garden, instead of three to four. They have three or four distinct planting seasons instead of one or two. They are faced with working with tenacious red clay or deep sand instead of dark, sandy loam. And they don't know how to verbalize it, but the sun isn't where they are accustomed to seeing it at various hours of the day. Worst of all, the old familiar flowers from gardens north of the Mason-Dixon line seem to melt away when planted on Memorial Day.

I'll Get By (with a little help from my friends)

Don't worry, you'll survive the transition, but there is no need to gut it out by yourself. Ask for help. The first place you need to visit is the Cooperative Extension Service office that serves your county. You may have to search through phone books to find the address. It really isn't a conspiracy to hide from the gardening public, and they aren't having an identity crisis. Sometimes they are listed under the name of the land grant university of the state: Texas A&M, North Carolina State University, Louisiana State University, Clemson University, or University of Kentucky, for example. If you don't find them there, look under Cooperative Extension Service, or Agricultural Extension Service, or plain old Extension Service. Explain that you are a home gardener and would like to come by and pick up bulletins on flowers, vegetables, landscaping, and pest control. You may have to pay a modest price for them, but they are well worth it. Don't be put off if you see all sorts of recommendations for chemical controls for garden pests. They are projections from uses on commercial crops. Slowly but surely, the extension specialists are beginning to offer alternatives to toxic chemicals, such as botanical and biological controls, and are promoting disease-resistant varieties.

Master Gardening Classes

Ask the Cooperative Extension Service how to go about signing up for their next Master Gardening class. Don't be misled by the name. You don't have to be a master of gardening to take the course. You just have to be willing to invest about twenty evenings or afternoons, learning all aspects of gardening from the ground up. Courses typically cost about a hundred dollars, but you can save that much in time and materials you might waste while floundering around, trying to learn on your own. The demand for space in the classes is so strong that some states have waiting lists two or three years ahead. Some rural counties don't offer Master Gardening courses, and a few states shot themselves in the foot a while back by cutting off university specialists who were teaching Master Gardening classes. Once you are certified as a Master Gardener you will be required to put in about as many hours of volunteer work as you put into study, but it is fun. The fellowship in local and state Master Gardening groups is as close and supportive as you'll find anywhere.

Lectures, Demonstrations, and Classes at Botanical Gardens and Retail Garden Centers

Every major city and most towns of middle size have at least one botanical garden or estate garden, and all have long-established retail garden centers. They reach out to help newcomers and novices as well as experienced gardeners. Look in the yellow pages under "botanical gardens" or "arboreta," or ask a senior sales associate at a retail garden center where to find the nearest one. Go to your library and check out *Gardening by Mail* (see Appendix). It has the names and addresses of major botanical gardens under "horticultural libraries." Most botanical gardens have ongoing programs of evaluating plants and distributing publications on what, when, and how to plant. Many also conduct guided tours of their gardens to introduce newcomers and visitors to the plants in their landscape and their conservatory (greenhouse).

TV and Radio Gardening Programs

For many years, *The Victory Garden* and Ed Hume's program, *Gardening in America*, both seen over PBS, were the only nationally broadcast TV gardening shows. But have things changed! With the advent of the Home and Garden TV channel, several crackerjack garden shows are being aired. All of them are scripted for a national audience. Some of the major metro areas have local TV garden shows, usually hosted by a horticultural agent from the Extension Service.

One of the best sources for gardening information, if you can tolerate the commercials, are radio gardening programs. They are often broadcast from 6:30 A.M. until 9:30 A.M. on Saturdays, and are set up for call-ins. The host is usually a horticulturist at a local garden center, an Extension Service specialist, or a newspaper columnist with a good following. When my old friend and fellow horticulturist Herb Lester was hosting a Saturday morning gardening program over a Nashville station, he asked me to come in as a guest. It was during the fall season. I don't know how it happened, but the talk got around to persimmons and paw paws, which led to tall stories about possums. We started getting calls from way down in Mississippi and Alabama, and way over in east Tennessee, in the richest array of country accents, telling the doggonedest stories you can imagine. What a morning that was!

Plant Societies

If along the way you fall in love with a particular species or genus of flowers, you may find a local chapter of a plant society in a town near you. *Gardening by Mail* has the names and addresses of the national headquarters of all the specialty plant societies: roses, daylilies, hostas, irises, herbs, peonies, lilacs, conifers, bonsai, rock garden plants, and so on. They can tell you where and how to contact the nearest chapter of their society. Some major cities have horticultural societies where hobbyists from various plant specialties come to pick up new information and to swap ideas.

Books

State gardening books are few and far between, but are increasing in number. Often, they are displayed in racks of books of local or regional interest, on a number of subjects. Taylor Publishing Company, which was of great assistance to me in publishing this book, has published several southern gardening books (see Appendix).

State books are a good place for newcomers or beginners to start, but they can't fully take the place of nationally distributed books that address certain plant specialties in depth. Look for titles by American authors. Think twice before buying a book by a British author. Even if the text has been "Americanized" by a writer over here, it can't come to grips with our peculiar soils and weather, and British books often picture and describe varieties or cultivars that aren't available over here. I have many British books in my library, but they are encyclopedias of specialty plants that help me research obscure species.

Internet and CDs

The Internet is not the best place for a newcomer to the South or a beginning gardener to start accumulating local information. I will repeat what I said in chapter 1: *Our special conditions demand special plants.* Except for information from your state land grant agricultural university, most of the data you get from the Internet will have been generated somewhere outside of the South. Some of it will be vague or too general, edited by people who don't understand seeds, plants, soils, the dynamics of water, or even elementary chemistry. On the other hand, a few will know gardening and landscaping thoroughly, including gardening in ways to minimize environmental impact. And there are some comprehensive and reliable CDs (see Appendix).

But how is a newcomer to the South or a beginner to distinguish between the qualified expert and the wannabe, or how to spot the zealot who does his best to swing everyone within his reach into his radical orbit? You'll learn, but to avoid being led into a thicket of misinformation, start with southern specialists who, like Michael Dirr and Allan Armitrage, have traveled widely and who have had years of experience in teaching and in writing authoritative books and CDs. Every land grant university has at least one or two specialists of this kind in its schools of horticulture or landscape architecture.

Seed and Plant Catalogs

Years ago, I read a survey which indicated that home gardeners received much of their gardening information from seed packets and seed and plant catalogs. They still do, but not as much as a generation ago. The difference is due to the gradual shift from direct-seeding in the garden or starting seeds indoors to buying bedding plants or potted perennials.

Many mail-order seed companies, large and small, have disappeared through mergers or purchases. Some have changed ownership but retained their good trade names. A few have ridden out the storm and prospered, and a handful of new startup companies have made it. The mainline seed companies have survived and grown by astute choices of new varieties and by modern management practices.

When I lived in the North, I relied on the catalog from Stokes Seeds, in Buffalo, New York, for information on varieties and their culture. Their catalog directions were as thorough as you will find in any textbook, and a lot easier to understand. Now, I rely on seed catalogs from Geo. W. Park Seed Co. as well. They are heavy on color. A relative newcomer, Territorial Seed Company, has some of the best cultural information I've seen in years on vegetable growing. For information on woody and herbaceous plants I use the catalog from Wayside Gardens; the big, thick catalog from ForestFarm (inquire about its price); and the specialized catalog from Woodlanders on woody plants for zones 8 and further south. There are many other good catalogs, but I can usually find what I need in these.

Now, several southern mail-order companies specializing in plants of herbs, hardy perennials, and native species are distributing catalogs. I particularly like the audacious catalog from Plant Delights Nursery, published by Tony and Michelle Avent. They are active in introducing new species from plant explorations, and new hybrids from plant breeders. These smaller companies are knowledgeable about the adaptability of the various cultivars to southern climates and don't try to stretch the parameters to sell more plants.

Hang Around Retail Garden Centers

This may sound like a zany idea, but it works. When you can spare a morning on a weekend, hang around a local garden center, reading plant labels and information on packages of products. Tell whoever is in charge who you are and what you are doing, so they won't conclude that you are either an incredibly dense thief or a clandestine shopper working for a competitor. Just stay out of the way of shoppers while you are taking notes. After two or three visits, you will begin to know the plants well enough to identify them without looking at labels. You may not have learned the products all that well, but at least you will know where to find them and what they are used for.

Don't Get So Hung Up on Summer That You Neglect the Other Seasons

You will hear a lot of talk about our many planting seasons but practically speaking, we plant most of our flowers, shrubs, and trees in the spring or fall. As soon as the winter rains subside and the frost-free date is past, it is time to plant summer flowers, and as soon as possible after summer heat has lost its punch, we plant flowers for winter color, also trees and shrubs. I wish we gardeners in zones six and seven had more choices than ornamental cabbage, *Primula veris*, pansies, violas, the hellebores, and winter-blooming bulbs and shrubs for cold-weather color, but that's the size of it. I suppose we should glory in what we can grow, rather than envying gardeners in zone 8 and further south.

Don't Push the Envelope on Planting Dates

Summer is not a good time for setting out flower plants or shrubs in the South, unless you can rig some sort of structure to shade the plants until they can send out roots into the surrounding soil. I had A-frames built of teakwood, hinged with stainless steel fittings, and sat them over herbaceous plants and small shrubs that I planted during hot weather.

They looked so much like chicken coops that I expected to see a mama hen and her biddies scratching around in the mulch, but they did the job, and kept the voracious deer away from the plants, at least temporarily. I may seem to be exaggerating the effect of our hot sun and dry summer weather on transplants, but I have lost more plants to the effects of late planting than from any other reason.

Ornamental banana trees in North Augusta, South Carolina

Brazilian button bush (*Centratherum punctatum*)

Limestone path.
WILLIAM D. ADAMS

Periwinkle (*Catharanthus roseus* 'Pretty in Pink')
PARK HORTICULTURAL TRIALS

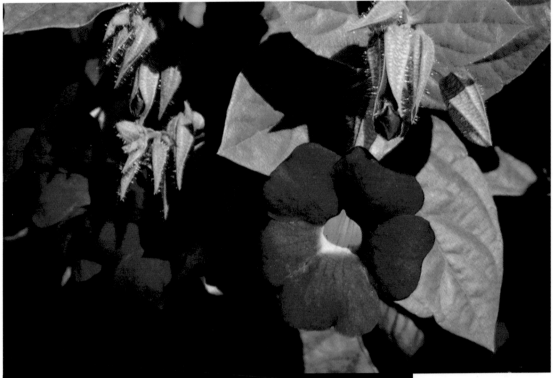

Blue clock vine *(Thunbergia grandiflora)*, Ball Horticultural trials

Red hot poker *(Kniphofia uvaria)*, Long Beach Estate, near Ashburton,
New Zealand

Verbena rigida, grown from seeds collected on a roadside near the Wilson home

Lamb's ear (*Stachys byzantina*) mature plant, Callaway Gardens, Pine Mountain, Georgia

Carolina jessamine at a southern site (*Gelsemium sempervirens*)

Spreading heliotrope (*Heliotropium amplexicaule*) in Wilson garden

Daylily (*Hemerocallis* 'Stella de Oro') in Waller, Texas
WILLIAM D. ADAMS

Fountain with red *Pentas lanceolata*, San Antonio Botanical Garden

Strawflower (*Helichrysum* 'Golden Beauty') planted in a basin, seated securely in a round wrought iron plant stand

The recently introduced bush *Pandorea jasminoides* 'Southern Belle' has not been extensively tested in the South, but should overwinter in zone 9 and south. Especially grown for this photo by Weidner's Greenhouses.

Handmade lightweight concrete (hypertufa) containers at Ashburton, New Zealand, show the patina of algae that comes with a few years of use. These containers are especially good for displaying perennials, as they can be left outdoors during winter without damage from freezing and thawing.

Croton (*Codiaeum variegatum*). Young plant growing in a container, San Antonio, Texas

THREE

What Gardeners Can Do to Minimize the Impact of Heat and Humidity

If you think you feel the heat and humidity on hot summer days, what about the plants in your garden? You can retreat to an air-conditioned interior, but they have to stay where you planted them. That's why choosing adapted cultivars, selecting appropriate sites, and preparing the soil for them is so important.

Start by Improving Your Soil

I've always thought of myself as a translator, positioned between sources of technical information on horticulture and home gardeners. I try to simplify the arcane terminology of scientists so that the average gardener can absorb it. Sometimes the result can be flat and dull, or God forbid, pedantic. Frankly, I wrestled with the opener for this section for a while, trying to avoid stock phrases. Horticulture is replete with concepts that have been boiled down into horticultural jargon. One or two words can be used describe a complicated process, such as, "Plants grow better in well-drained, well-aerated soil, containing 2 to 5 percent fine organic matter." Well, of course they do, unless they are swamp denizens! And, "Plants respond to such a healthy environment by forming strong, widespread root systems that can reach deep into the soil for moisture and plant nutrients." I can just hear you saying, "*I* knew that!"

But here's where cause and effect aren't so obvious. You have created a chicken/egg situation when you attribute good plant growth just to improved drainage, aeration, and soil structure and texture. Actually, much of the credit for good plant growth has to go to a healthy population of soil microorganisms doing their thing. They not only convert nutrients to forms that can be used by plants but also cause soil particles to clump together, which allows more oxygen to penetrate and drainage to proceed faster. So, everything you do to improve the soil physically, indirectly improves it biologically. Back when Rodale's magazine was called *Organic Gardening and Farming*, they reminded us often that you don't feed plants, you feed the soil. They meant feeding with compost or organic plant food, of course.

Feeding Your Soil (Fertilizing)

Good plant nutrition produces good root systems, providing you have limed and aerated the soil with organic matter. I'm not a purist when it comes to plant foods because both organic and processed mineral fertilizers seem to work equally well in my garden. I don't use much of either because after a few years of adding organic matter and mulching with pine bark, my soil makes efficient use of any nutrients I apply. Ever since my childhood, helping my father feed muskmelons and watermelons with cottonseed meal—a marvelous organic source of nitrogen with a little phosphorus and potash as well—I've appreciated the good job it does of feeding both vegetables and flowers. The analysis on the bag is not impressive, but don't let it dissuade you from buying it or other organic fertilizers. Fertilizer laws are written so that only the available fraction of the three major nutrient elements can be claimed. Cottonseed meal and other organic fertilizers have to be broken down by soil organisms before much of their nutrient content is released. You get more nutrients than you bargained for, and in this day and age, that's a switch!

You can also feed your flowers with granular or soluble crystalline fertilizers. Granular fertilizer works more efficiently if it is worked into the soil or dribbled into shallow furrows around plants and covered with soil. Contrary to what you might have read, the so-called "liquid fertilizers" are absorbed more from the soil than through the foliage. There is little point in hosing down the plants with a spray of liquid fertilizer. You can get more precise coverage by applying the fertilizer solution to the soil beneath the foliage canopy of plants, and you don't risk burning the leaves with a strong solution. It can happen quickly on a warm day when the temperature is rising.

In general, you need to fertilize plants more in the South than in the North, especially if your flower beds are on deep, sandy soil.

High heat and humidity and frequent rains tend to make fertilizers volatilize and lose their nitrogen fraction, while much of the phosphate and potash either leaches out of the reach of roots or is fixed in insoluble forms. Such conditions make a good case for the use of controlled-release fertilizers such as Osmocote or Polyon. Their nutrients gradually diffuse through a plastic membrane that surrounds each granule, and feeder roots have a better chance of absorbing the nutrient ions before they escape or are locked up.

Incorporating Organic Matter

Whether your soil is clay or sand or somewhere in between, it can benefit from your adding and turning-under organic matter. Not corn stalks or chunks of wood or bark, or raw sawdust (which can steal nitrogen needed for plant growth), but fine particles that soil organisms can surround and decompose. It can be mushroom compost, dried cow manure, a fine screen of pine bark, or composted wastes of several kinds. A generous application of a "soil conditioner" of this type can be expensive, so you may want to improve one flower bed at a time to soften the financial shock. Apply a two-inch layer of organic soil conditioner worked in as deeply as your spade can dig. You can do a more thorough job of mixing it in if you till or spade the soil before and after spreading the soil conditioner.

Adding Limestone

Almost every garden in the South can benefit from having limestone worked in to spade depth. The exceptions are where you, or the gardener before you, added limestone for several years to correct the soil pH, or where marine organisms created an alkaline sand that dominates your garden soil. Alkaline soils are as scarce as hens' teeth in the South, until you begin to encounter the blacklands or the caliche soil in Central and West Texas or South Florida limestone-based soils. Southern soils have been subjected to so many indignities for so many years that the scanty stores of calcium and magnesium they originally contained have long since been depleted. The result is acidic soils (low pH) with skewed levels of available micronutrients. (When the soil pH drops to 5.0 or lower, certain micronutrients become unavailable to plants, while others go off the charts in solubility.)

Now, before you rush out and purchase limestone, understand that you may find several kinds at your garden center. What you want is either finely ground or pelletized dolomitic limestone. Finely ground is less expensive than pelletized because the pellets are made by rolling fine particles in a sticky binder. That extra step costs you money, but it reduces the dust factor, which can be a nuisance on a windy day. Dolomitic limestone contains both calcium and magnesium, usually in about equal parts. Buy as big a bag as you can tote, because you're going to apply it at a rate of about two to five pounds per one hundred square feet.

Back in 1946, my soils professor told me that limestone has to be "incorporated in the soil, as it is relatively immobile." What he meant was that limestone stays where you put it. If you want it down in the root zone where feeder roots can suck it up, you're going to have to mix it thoroughly with the soil. Do it at the same time you are turning under and mixing in the organic soil conditioner. The safest approach is to have your soil tested every year or two by the Extension Service. Tests will tell you if your soil needs liming, and if so, how much to apply. Your flower beds may need liming every two or three years to maintain a desirable soil pH level of about 5.5 to 6.0.

When liming beds that have been mulched with pine, cypress, or hardwood bark, there's no need to dig-in the limestone. Just scatter it over the top of the mulch, preferably in the fall of the year. The tunneling of earthworms will carry much of it down into the root zone, and the network of hair roots at the interface of the mulch and the soil will absorb and translocate much of the remainder throughout the tissue of plants.

How about liming beds of azaleas, rhododendrons, and blueberries? Do it. Pay no attention to the folklore about "azaleas like acid soil." It is true that they don't care for alkaline soil, yet all the so-called "acid-loving" plants need a little calcium and magnesium, and they don't seem to react to a moderate rise in soil pH. Lime them per soil test recommendations, not to exceed pH 6.0. You will be amazed at how much better your azaleas and rhododendrons will look, and how much more bloom they will produce on very acid soils after liming.

Should You Add Sand to Clay Soils?

I hate it when I have to answer a question with, "It all depends." But there is sand, and there is sand. River sand, for example, can be loaded with weed seeds, and heaven knows which pollutants. You are better off using mined sand; it is much cleaner. "Builder's sand" can be either of the foregoing. If you order bulk sand, the dealer should be able to tell you whether it is mined or river sand. If he has no idea, look at it carefully. If the particles are all the same color, the chances are good that it is sand mined from ancient dunes. Just be sure your driveway pavement can bear the weight of a dump truck loaded with sand, and that you are up to the chore of wheel-barrowing load after load to the dumping point in your landscape.

PermaTill, a product made from heat-expanded slate, works better than sand as a soil conditioner. Always, when you add sand or PermaTill to clay soils, add an organic soil conditioner as well. Adding sand alone to clay soil will just create sandy mud or sandy bricks, depending on whether the soil is wet or dry. Yet, the combination of two inches of organic matter and an inch or two of clean, coarse sand can result in soil like you see on TV gardening programs! How about using Play Sand? No, keep it out of your garden. Some brands have been treated with a disinfectant to make it safe for kids to play in, but the disinfectant can kill plants.

Should You Add Clay to Sandy Soils?

No, or you will end up with sandy mud or sandy bricks. If clay were an actor, he would be called a "slippery character." When you mix clay with sand, the tiny laminar particles of clay slip down between the grains of sand and collect in a layer somewhere down below. That layer can become nearly impermeable, and can retard the up and down movement of water in the soil. The result will be poor drainage and impeded capillary action.

Then What Should You Add to Sandy Soils?

Organic matter and limestone; that's all. Once you have brought up the organic fraction in the soil to between 2 and 5 percent, you can keep it there by mulching your flower and shrub beds and around trees with pine, hardwood, or cypress bark. You will have to add (top dress) an inch or so every year thereafter because our long, hot summers and intensive irrigation accelerate the decomposition of organic matter. The effort and expense of applying organic soil conditioners and mulches will be justified, however, when you see how much better your soil will hold water, and how much more effective your fertilizer applications will be. Organic matter has the capacity to store water and plant nutrients in reserve; sand does not. Organic mulches reduce the amount of water lost to evaporation, and suppress weeds.

Should You Haul in Topsoil?

Stop and think about it for a moment, and you can dispel any doubt about the answer. "Topsoil" can be obtained from any place, and can contain everything from noxious weed seeds to residues of persistent herbicides such as soil sterilants. When you purchase topsoil, you are supporting the people who scalp it from subdivisions, malls, and parking-lots-to-be, and sell it to you. Unless you must have fill dirt to bring part of your lot up to grade, don't buy soil of any kind. Instead, improve what you already have by adding soil conditioners and perhaps coarse sand.

Should You Mulch?

Absolutely! Mulches of hardwood or pine bark (or, in the West, fir bark as well) suppress weeds, conserve moisture, and reduce soil splash. And they look good, certainly much better than bare soil. Mulches can be purchased by the bag or, in many places in the South, by the truckload. I mulched several flower and shrub beds around my home a few years ago, and I am very pleased with the way mulch has cut down on weeding and has reduced drought stress during our dry summers. I add more mulch each spring to replace that which decomposes to humus and finally oxidizes to nothing. I do not recommend using chipped wood as a landscape mulch. It tends to cause "nitrogen drawdown" in the soil, which results in yellowish foliage and poor growth. When spreading mulches, pull it away from tree trunks and the crowns of perennials to avoid causing trunk cankers or crown rot.

Should You Install an Irrigation System?

Only a few years down the road, that will be a moot question. There won't be sufficient water for us to waste it on keeping emerald-green, immaculate lawns. For now, the pressure for conforming to neighborhood standards is so great that you may have to install a sprinkler irrigation system, or have it done professionally. I don't water my farmhouse lawn. Never have, never will, but I don't live where a neighborhood committee or a city bureaucrat could force me to do it. I do mow my three-acre yard when the spirit moves me, mostly because our resident bluebirds won't feed where the grass is tall. I'm not afraid of the snakes and varmints that hide in tall grass, but they are.

When water use becomes more stringently regulated (and it will, sooner than later), species of grasses will be found that can stay passably green with little plant food and even less water. You will have to raise your mower to cut at a three-inch height. Lawns will look more pastoral than they do now, and will go through ups and downs in attractiveness, depending on rain. We will come to accept their shaggy appearance, and will like being freed from the guilt that comes with wasting a precious resource.

If you do put in a sprinkler system, buy directional heads that spray away from flower and shrub beds and the root zones of trees. Gradually increase the size of your beds and borders to decrease the amount of your yard that is under grass. I know that in the prairie states homeowners are converting entire yards (except for walks) to prairie gardens, but it won't work as well in the South, not even if it were practical to maintain native perennials with periodic burning. Our weed problem, especially with introduced grasses and broad-leafed winter weeds, is too severe.

While I am philosophically against sprinkler irrigation, I am a fan of drip irrigation for tree and shrub borders. Drip systems economize on water and deliver water to where it is needed, even when the wind is blowing strongly. You can use drip systems to irrigate beds of widely-spaced perennial plants, but they aren't practical for closely-spaced annuals. Plants shouldn't be more than nine inches away from the emitter or their roots can't reach the narrow cone of water that leaks from it. For my annual flower beds I hook a hose to an oscillating Rainbird impulse sprinkler atop a tall tripod that lifts it above the tallest flowers. I water during morning hours so the warming sun will dry the foliage. I water my flower and shrub beds once every seven to ten days during dry spells. My clay soil holds water fairly well, and all my beds are mulched to reduce water lost to evaporation. On deep, sandy soils, more frequent watering is called for.

How Can You Reduce the Impact of Periodic Dry Spells and Prolonged Droughts?

This may sound contradictory, but raised beds can reduce the stress factor, if you mix organic matter into the soil to elevate it. Raised, organically-fortified soil absorbs water better than native clay. Modified clay drains better and modified sand holds moisture better. Both enjoy improved aeration. Everything works together to promote better root growth, which in turn enables plants to better withstand weather stresses. Mulches also help a great deal, of course. There are some drastic steps you can take as well, such as driving a sharpened spade to full depth around your flower beds. Tree roots can travel unexpectedly long distances to rob your flower beds of water and plant nutrients. Root pruning has only a temporary effect, and will have to be repeated yearly.

Of all the things you can do to help your flowers, deep watering is the most important. If water from a sprinkler begins to run off a flower bed in an hour or less, move the sprinkler to another spot, and bring it back later, after the first watering has soaked in. Deep watering moistens the soil profile down deep, encouraging plant roots to grow down instead of proliferating near the surface. Set a water glass near your sprinkler and let it accumulate at least two inches of water. On clay soils, two inches of water should penetrate to a depth of ten inches or so, perhaps twice that deep on sand. Technically, most flowers can get by on one inch of water per week from either rainfall or irrigation, but shallow watering can encourage the formation of roots near the surface of the soil.

How Can You Moisten Spots That Always Stay Dry?

The easiest way to rectify such problems is to buy a horticultural surfactant from your garden center. They may have to order it for you. It is basically a mild detergent that makes water wetter, and is not toxic to plants. Mix it with water according to directions and sprinkle or spray it on the dry spot. You may have to repeat the application two or three times, watering between each application. Once the water has penetrated through the compacted soil, it should absorb water from a sprinkler for two or three weeks before needing another application of surfactant. If the surfactant doesn't work, you may have an obstruction in the soil, like masonry rubble or waste cement buried by builders, or something as simple as compaction by machinery during the construction of your home, which caused an impervious layer called "hardpan" several inches down in the soil profile. You may wish to dig a hole and look for what is causing the dry spot. Of course, you may be unlucky enough to find a boulder as big as a refrigerator, which either has to be skidded out or left in place to confound the next person to own your home. So, get out the pickaxe, shovel, and wheelbarrow; you've a big job ahead of you.

How Can You Use Shade to the Best Advantage?

One of the first acts of a southerner when faced with a new garden-to-be is to set out shade trees. Southern sun is no fun from midsummer until the colors turn. Trees not only give gardeners relief from direct sunlight; they also give flowering plants a break. They create patterns of sun and shade, change the ambiance of landscapes, and lift your eyes up from ground level. Broad-leafed evergreen or needle-leafed conifers can protect semi-hardy plants from frost, if they are planted beneath the shelter of the limbs.

Yet, that first step of planting shade trees is often a misstep. Trees that grow too large for the landscape are a common mistake, or trees that have genetic weaknesses like the Bradford pears that tend to self-destruct upon reaching ten to fifteen years of age. Still, the most common mistake is one of omission rather than commission. Lacking sufficient information, gardeners buy trees that don't give them much bang for their buck. You can buy trees that mature at a rather small size, flower in the spring, turn color in the fall, and bear berries to feed wild birds. Some even serve as host plants for butterflies. A book I wrote with Guy Sternberg, *Landscaping with Native Trees*, is a good place to check before sallying forth to buy trees.

You have to work with what you've got; that we all know. Let's say that you or the gardener who had the property before you planted trees that are casting dense shade and creating intense root competition. It is well-nigh impossible to grow any flowers beneath or near their canopies. The first step is to limb-up the trees, sparing *Magnolia grandiflora* and the conifers, which look better with branches to the ground. Either read up on how to do it safely (safe to the tree as well as to you) or call in a certified arborist. Removing lower limbs by limbing-up will allow more sun to illuminate the area beneath the canopy of foliage.

Shade Structures

Let's face it. During the summer, our problem in southern gardens is too much sun rather than too little. That excess can kill or stunt plants. You can almost hear them crying for relief. You might give the suffering ones relief with a structure like the "ramadas" of southern New Mexico and Arizona. We would call them "lath houses." They cast 50 percent shade, but that percentage is lessened by sunlight that bounces in from surrounding areas. They are somewhat more practical for sheltering sun-sensitive plants than gazebos, which have solid roofs. I've seen curved pergolas at estates where money was no object, constructed of heavy treated timbers on concrete piers to last for years. Latticework panels are sometimes included to display small vines such as standard clematis. Lath structures create lots of opportunities for hanging baskets and for staging containers of shade-tolerant flowers, as well as running room for vines.

The happiest feature of shade structures is that they don't have roots that compete with small plants, as do trees. However, trees are nature's own shade structures. You can go around the problem of root competition by setting containers beneath tree canopies, or hanging baskets of flowers from limbs.

Eliminate Competing Weeds

If you build it, they will come . . . weeds, that is. They will pop up in the most elaborate flower beds in the ritziest neighborhood as well as in a strip of rose moss plants bordering a driveway to a cottage. "Where do they come from?" is a frequent question. They come from the soil, of course, where they may have been dropped years ago. Weeds and their seeds are survivors.

Weeds compete with flowers and shrubs for soil moisture and plant nutrients, and it isn't a fair fight. Weeds grow faster and often larger than flowers. You need to pull or hoe them while they are small, and certainly before they form seeds. You need to space your flowers fairly closely so they grow together and shade out the weed seeds that need sun to germinate. Yet, you don't want to cram flowers so close together that they compete strongly with each other. Think of them as little people who, when they grow up, can reach out and touch the fingertips of their neighbors without invading their space.

How Can You Know Whether a Plant Is Well Grown?

Poorly-grown or potbound plants or flowers will never develop a strong root system and will look puny the rest of their lives. They may even give up the ghost during a hot, dry spell. But how do you know if a plant has been well grown and is at or near its prime? Look at its general color first, then for sturdy stems, not spindly and sparsely leafed. Turn the plant upside down and check the undersides of the leaves for tiny insects such as spider mites or aphids. (I was shopping in a garden center one day when I saw a load of tropical plants that had just been delivered and were sitting on the floor, waiting to be loaded on the shelves. Noticing that they looked distressed, I checked the leaves and found that they were loaded with aphids. I found the manager and told him what I had seen. Believe me, those plants were rushed out of the building in a jiffy, before they contaminated the rest of the stock. I wouldn't have wanted to be in the shoes of the grower when that dealer phoned him!) Well, such things happen, and plants can be neglected or allowed to stay for too long in small pots or packs, so it is up to you to kick the tires before buying.

It is okay to tap a plant out of a pot and inspect its root system. Do it carefully, because some may have been potted up so recently that the network of feeder roots will be fragile. If the plant is badly rootbound, with roots winding round and round the bottom of the pot, don't buy it. Even if you could straighten and spread out the roots when setting the plant in the garden, most of the root hairs will have been rubbed off or damaged. That plant would be slow about replacing its damaged roots, and would never catch up with a younger plant without congested roots.

After you have set out flowers in your garden, position a sprinkler in the flower bed and let it soak the soil thoroughly. Water again in a day or two, and again two days later. So many gardeners set out plants and give them a brief blessing of water from a hose, then forget about them. Dry weather sets in before the plants can send roots into the surrounding soil to extract water, and when the gardener finally takes note of their suffering, it is too late to save them. It has happened to me, when I have set out plants in an isolated bed and forgotten about them. I hate it when it happens. Plants can't holler at you to get your attention; you have to set up a routine for watering new transplants and follow it religiously.

FOUR

Growing Flowers and Herbs in Containers

During the past three decades I've watched growing plants in containers become a major trend in home horticulture. It is strongest in the South and the West, largely because where winters are mild, gardeners can grow flowers in containers year-round without protection. It isn't a fad, because properly planted and staged containers can add a whole new dimension to landscapes.

In my lecture titled "Landscaping with Container Plants," I tell my audiences that growing plants in containers is neither easier nor more difficult than growing them in the ground—only different. Everything the plant needs has to come from the gardener, because plants can't send out roots to get what they need to grow and develop, as they can in ground beds. The nutrient reserve and the supply of soil moisture is limited to what the soil in the container can hold, which means that garden soils, no matter how good they are, are not suitable for use in containers. They dry out and shrink away from the sides of the container, making it difficult to wet the rootball. Also, southern heat, humidity, and cloudbursts can stress flowers grown through the summer in containers, which must be taken into consideration when you are selecting plants and containers, and deciding where to place them.

Potting Soils

The best potting soils have no real soil in them. Yet, while they are man-made, they are formulated with mostly natural products. They are designed to retain moisture without becoming waterlogged and to hold a desirable amount of plant nutrients and moisture in reserve. But most important, they remain well-aerated without becoming too dry to support a wide range of plant species. The best potting soils for growing flowers and herbs out-of-doors drain moderately fast, resulting in good aeration. In the South, they are usually composed of about three parts of properly aged and screened pine bark and one part high-quality Canadian sphagnum peat moss. They are fortified with enough limestone to take plants through the summer, and premium grades of potting soils contain a long-lasting, controlled-release fertilizer as well. Such potting soils are usually light in weight, and like a sponge, retain their structure throughout the growing season.

Other potting soils can contain muck (sedge or wood peat), sand, topsoil, manure, municipal compost, sawmill wastes, and other unpredictable components. Such soils are almost always quite heavy for their volume and tend to drain slower than is desirable for outdoor use. Some of the ultra-fine particles such as those of muck can slip down to the bottom of the container and collect in a soggy layer that can rot roots.

Perlite (white, heat-expanded silica) and vermiculite (glittery, heat-expanded mica) are sometimes added to outdoor potting soils. Perlite is structurally strong and works to improve aeration, but the particles of vermiculite are so fragile that they can crush under the weight of a large volume of soil. Vermiculite works best as a component of potting soils for growing houseplants and for starting seedlings. Potting mixes for small pots and for house plants are usually more dense and slower-draining than those designed for outdoor containers.

The best way to select a good potting soil for outdoor use is to ask the dealer for a pine bark and sphagnum peat moss mixture of the type his nursery uses for potting up plants in large containers. Then, turn over the package and read the statement of contents on the reverse side. It could be very instructive.

Supplementary Limestone and Plant Nutrients

Regardless of the quality of the potting soil, I would recommend mixing in one-eighth of a cup of dolomitic limestone per gallon of mix. The limestone should be either powdered or pelletized so it can begin working immediately. Avoid coarse agricultural limestone; it releases so slowly that it is ineffective in containers. Dolomitic limestone contains calcium and magnesium, and serves as a source of these two important secondary nutrients as well as an agent for taking the edge off the natural acidity of the potting soil. Incorporating

limestone is especially important when you are growing fruiting vegetables in containers, as it can help prevent the condition known as
blossom end rot. Out where the West begins, and where the tap
water is very hard, it may not be necessary to add limestone to your
potting soil. Indeed, limestone may be virtually impossible to find
locally in western states. Hard water is due to the presence of minerals
such as calcium and magnesium, and sometimes sodium.

Mixing controlled-release fertilizer into potting soil before planting is also a good idea, but first read the statement of contents on the
back of the package. Premium-quality potting soils may have been
already fortified with long-lasting fertilizer, and nothing will be
gained by doubling up on it. Never add common granular lawn or
garden fertilizer to potting mixes. They can release enough ammonia
to harm feeder roots or can damage roots by their high salt content.

How Often Should You Feed Plants in Containers?

If your potting mix contains long-lasting, controlled-release fertilizer,
or if you added it according to directions, you may not need to add
any additional fertilizer until late summer. It depends on the particular product. Some controlled-release pellets have a thick coating of
vinyl or polyethylene and will feed for seven to nine months under
southern conditions. Others have thinner jackets and will feed for
three to four months.

For guidance, read the statement on the back of the package. If
your plants begin to look puny in late summer, swirl more controlled-release fertilizer into the top two or three inches of potting
mix. Such fertilizers always work better if they are mixed with the soil
rather than spread on the surface.

You may prefer to liquid-feed your plants by dissolving a
crystalline fertilizer in water or by diluting an organic fertilizer such
as fish emulsion according to directions. It usually takes only one
experience with ready-to-use liquid fertilizers to convince a gardener
that buying and diluting a concentrate is the more economical way to
go. Be prepared to feed weekly with liquid fertilizers. The frequent
watering and heavy rainstorms in the South conspire to leach fertilizers down and out the drain hole. Pour liquid fertilizers on the soil
around plants rather than spraying them on the foliage.

When you liquid-feed your outdoor plants in containers, the
analysis (N–P–K content) isn't all that important. However, to
encourage flowering, you may wish to switch from a balanced analysis
such as 20–20–20 to something like 15–30–15 when flower buds begin

to form. The slightly lower nitrogen content should act to minimize vegetative growth while the higher phosphate would help to maximize flower production.

What Are Micronutrients and Should You Use Them?

Most soluble fertilizers for liquid feeding and some controlled-release fertilizers contain micronutrients such as iron, manganese, copper, cobalt, boron, molybdenum, and zinc. The secondary nutrients such as calcium, magnesium, and sulfur are usually present in the limestone and gypsum added to high-quality potting mixes by the manufacturer.

The two nutrient deficiencies most likely to occur in container-grown plants are iron and calcium. Iron deficiency rarely shows up in the South. When it does, you can correct it with chelated (sequestered) iron. Calcium deficiency is easy to rectify with powdered limestone or liquid lime. Nutrient deficiencies, and especially those of micronutrients, are difficult for home gardeners to diagnose. Take a slip of the affected plant to a long-established local garden center and ask an experienced associate to identify the problem and suggest a solution. Some Extension Service offices are staffed by Master Gardeners who are good at helping with plant nutrition problems.

Deficiencies of major and minor nutrients are more likely to occur with container plants than with those growing in the ground, especially late in the growing season, or after a plant has become rootbound. The Cooperative Extension Service of the State of Virginia has published a useful table, "A Guide to Diagnosing Nutrient Deficiencies by Foliar Symptoms," publication 430-018. It contains the most concise information I've seen to help gardeners make educated guesses at what their plants are trying to tell them. The table appears on page 34, reprinted with permission.

By the way, more problems are caused by micronutrient toxicity than by deficiencies. Have the plant problem diagnosed before concluding that micronutrients are needed. To give you an idea of the minuscule amount of a micronutrient needed to correct a deficiency in soil, the usual recommendation to correct a boron deficiency is two pounds of boron per acre! How would you like the job of scattering two pounds of boron uniformly over an area of 43,560 square feet?

You may have seen TV commercials demonstrating spraying liquid fertilizers on the foliage of flowers and shrubs, and may have

Symptoms appear in older leaves first:	Indicated deficiency

General chlorosis followed by necrosis
(tissue death) and leaf drop; overall
growth stunted .... **NITROGEN**

Marginal chlorosis followed by interveinal
chlorosis; tips and margins may become
brittle, curl upward, and die ....**MAGNESIUM**

General, then marginal, then interveinal
chlorosis; leaf margins may curl
or roll, then die ....**MOLYBDENUM**

Interveinal tip chlorosis, then necrosis;
leaf margins may become brown
and curl downward..**POTASSIUM**

Leaves develop blue-green or red-purple
coloration, possibly yellowing ....**PHOSPHORUS**

Symptoms appear in youngest leaves first:

Light green to yellowing, interveinal
area even lighter ....**SULFUR**

Veins green, distinctive interveinal chlorosis
yellow or white, leaf drop if severe ....**IRON**

Smallest veins green, interveinal chlorosis
beginning at margins progressing to midribs,
followed by interveinal necrotic spots............................**MANGANESE**

Very small, stiff, chlorotic or mottled leaves;
shortened internodes causing rosetting ....**ZINC**

Terminal wilting, chlorosis, rosetting and death;
veins lighter than interveinal areas..**COPPER**

Terminal buds die:

Lateral buds and root tips also die, or
lateral growth has few leaves that are
chlorotic or necrotic, small, brittle,
thick and cupped downward ....**BORON**

Tips distorted or die back; young leaves
chlorotic, hard, stiff, margins distorted...............................**CALCIUM**

concluded that plants take up nutrients through their foliage. What the commercials don't tell you is that the plants are absorbing virtually all of the plant nutrients from the fertilizer that drips on the soil below the plants. Very little of the nutrient content in fertilizers is taken up through the leaves or stems of plants. One of the few situations where foliar feeding is recommended for commercial floral crops is to correct severe micronutrient deficiencies. Enough of the deficient nutrient can penetrate leaves to stave off death long enough for the plant to take up more through the roots. But application rates are so critical it might be safer for home gardeners to correct the deficiency by the slower means of drenching the root zone with a solution containing the desired micronutrient.

How Often Should You Water?

It depends on the weather. In cloudy or rainy weather: only when potting soil feels dry to the touch. During hot, windy weather: once or twice a day. When you are faced with watering several containers daily during hot, dry weather, you begin looking for ways to prolong the interval between waterings. One of the best ways is by mixing an absorbent with your potting soil, especially if it is going to be used in a hanging basket. Absorbents resemble little granules of gelatin, and they have the capacity to hold many times their weight in water. When used as directed, absorbents can sustain plants through perhaps a day or two of neglect, but they can't work miracles. They are sold under several brand names.

Gardeners who can't be home every day should investigate installing a drip irrigation system with spaghetti tubes and individual drop heads for each container. Programmable controls can now be purchased at reasonable prices. They can be set to water for as long as you wish and whenever you wish. It is also possible to set a container inside a larger one and stuff around and beneath it with long-fiber sphagnum moss. The moss will help to insulate against heat driving through the side walls, and will serve as a water reservoir. I've seen some gardeners paint their containers white to increase reflectivity and to decrease heat absorption. It does work!

Each time you water, see that water runs out the drainage hole. If you think you are saving water by applying so little that none runs out the hole, you are doing the plant a disservice. The drainage water will take excess salts out with it that could otherwise accumulate and hurt plant roots.

Types of Containers

Visit a big garden center or a pottery specialist such as Craven Pottery in Commerce, Georgia, and you will see not only terra-cotta clay containers in all sizes and shapes, but faux terra-cotta (PVC plastic) containers, wood, concrete, and perhaps fiberglass. The PVC containers cost less than clay and dry out more slowly, but are not quite as attractive. When selecting containers, start with sizes of five to seven gallons and up. Smaller containers dry out too fast, especially strawberry jars and hanging baskets which have a comparatively large surface area for evaporation. Concrete is the most durable material but is very heavy and tends to absorb heat and dry out potting soils and roots.

Coming on the market now are hypertufa containers made of lightweight concrete. You can make them by mixing one part Portland cement (no sand or gravel) with two parts each (by volume) of peat moss and either perlite or vermiculite. For strength, you can add to the mortar short pieces of strong fiber called FiberMesh and a concrete hardener called Acril 60. You can usually find them at builders' supply stores, but if not, look for them at an outlet for concrete supplies and decorative stone. Make a stiff mortar with water, and plaster it one and one-half to two inches deep inside or outside of a mold. Remove the container from the mold after twenty-four hours and let it cure in the shade. Sprinkle it frequently. Cover it with plastic to retard drying and to improve curing. Continued curing allows the composite to harden while rains leach out some of the alkalinity in the concrete. Be sure to provide for drainage holes.

Selecting a Choice Site for a Container

You can set containers in full sun in the South, but they dry out distressingly fast. Better you should set them where they can get afternoon shade. One of the best places for them is just inside the drip line of trees, where they can get a mixture of sun and shade. If shade is from a structure, afternoon shade is preferred. Containers give you a way to have colorful flowers in areas where root competition for plant nutrients and water would complicate growing flowers in the ground. If you plan to set a container where it will get light to moderate shade, be sure to plant it with flowers known to tolerate shade without growing leggy.

Use Your Expensive Real Estate Every Month of the Year

People in my audiences look at me strangely when I refer to the "expensive real estate" in containers. All costs considered, it is. So why not do what the farmers call "succession cropping"? Plant bulbs in your containers in the fall, and when they have sprouted, set pansy, viola, ornamental cabbage, or *Primula veris* plants between them. After the bulbs and winter flowers have done their thing, set plants of heat-resistant summer flowers among them. You can even interplant fall asters or chrysanthemums when the summer flowers have begun to fade. If you plant bulbs in containers late in the year, use one of concrete or hypertufa to avoid damage by freezing and thawing.

Don't forget the herbs! They are ready-made for growing in containers. If you are serious about including herbs in your salads, desserts, and cooked dishes, plant containers with herbs and set them in a sunny spot by the door to your kitchen. Not having to slog through the mud and dew to a distant herb garden will assure that when a recipe calls for a pinch of this and a soupçon of that, you will have it at your fingertips!

Should Potting Soils Be Reused?

I recommend dumping potting soils after each growing season. Spent soils make a good mulch or soil conditioner for flower beds. After a long, hard season of use, the fine particles in potting mixes will have largely disappeared, due to oxidation and the activity of feeder roots. The remainder will be rather coarse and will drain faster than is desirable.

In addition, salts may have accumulated, and additives such as limestone and gypsum will have been used up. Out of balance physically and chemically, the spent potting mix can no longer perform well.

Which brings up the question: if you grow successive crops, when is the best time to stop, dump the old mix, and refill the container with new potting soil, fortified with dolomitic limestone and perhaps controlled-release fertilizer? I would do it in the spring, after the bulbs have bloomed and before the summer annuals begin their long tenancy. Plants grow slowly during the fall and winter season and don't demand as much from soils and plant nutrients as summer crops.

❧ FIVE ❧

American Horticultural Society (AHS) Plant Heat-Zone Map

by Marc Cathey, Ph.D.

This recently published map is the product of many years' research by Dr. Marc Cathey, President Emeritus of AHS, in cooperation with nursery-men, botanical gardens, arboreta, and amateur plant specialists all over the country. The map is divided into zones calculated on the average number of days per year of temperatures above 86°F (30°C). That part of this work-in-progress is done. What remains to be completed is the massive job of determining the heat-zone adaptability for each plant species, and in some instances, each cultivar. Dr. Cathey told me in 1999 that they had already established plant heat-zone parameters for twenty thousand cultivars. You can order the two-by-three-foot poster map by phoning the AHS (see Appendix). Dr. Cathey's companion book, *Heat Zone Gardening*, can be purchased in bookstores nationally.

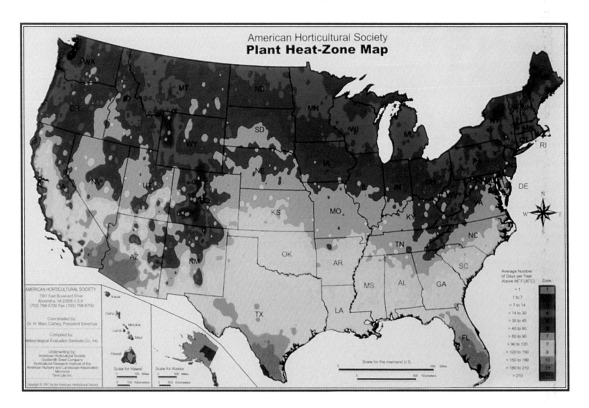

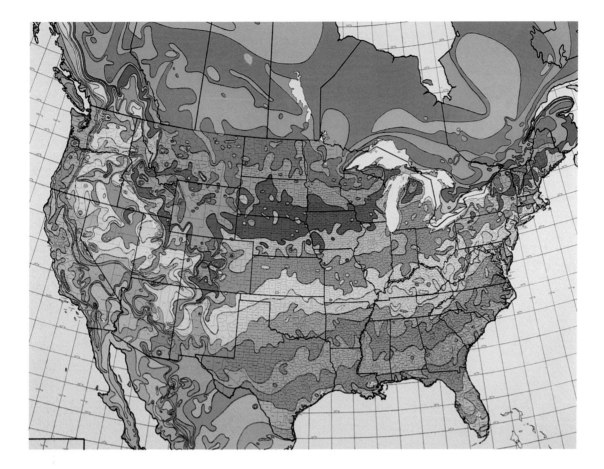

USDA Plant Hardiness Zone Map
(Revised Version)

This map, courtesy of the Agricultural Research Service, USDA, has been of great value to professional growers and home gardeners for many years. It is divided into zones by average minimum winter temperatures experienced over a long period of time. Most plant species and cultivars have been given USDA hardiness zone ratings gathered from reports sent in from many cooperators. The first edition lacked hardiness zone 11, which prevails in the tropical parts of Mexico and the Caribbean.

Jim Wilson's Favorite Flowers for Southern Summers

So many factors can influence the growth of flowers that the specifications given for plants should be considered approximations. Plant height and spread can vary not only with soil fertility, length of growing season, and the amount and distribution of water, but also with planting time. Often, early-planted flowers have the time to develop good-sized frames before their growth is slowed by the burden of supporting flowers and by intense heat. Shade can affect the size of sun-loving flowers. In some cases, plants will grow larger and fill out better if given light shade in the afternoon, which reduces stress caused by strong sunlight.

Shade restricts the home gardener's choice of flowers much more in the North than in the South. Many kinds that need full sun in the North will thrive in afternoon shade in the South. Not many flowering species will grow in moderate shade in the South, and even fewer will thrive and flower in dense shade. This is due partly to root competition from the trees that cast the shade, which explains why containers of the same flowers will grow better under similarly shaded conditions. They escape root competition from trees (but only if you elevate them on bricks or blocks). In general, shade-tolerant plants will suffer if planted in full sun. They evolved in shaded habitats and tend to wilt and scorch in the intense sun of mid to late afternoon. Their roots can't take up water as fast as their leaves transpire it.

You won't find several of the most popular flowers for the Midsouth and Upper South on this list, especially annuals. They are richly described in nearly every catalog and in garden books. Most gardeners grew up with them. Instead, this list is composed mostly of flowers that are well known in the lower South for their resistance to heat and humidity, and that are gradually making their way into markets further north. You will find only a few flowers on this list that are customarily planted in the fall for winter and early spring bloom, and none of the cool-weather species that are spring-planted in the North. However, you will find *a treasure trove of flowers that, when spring-planted in the South, will bloom through most or all of the summer months,* either in ground beds or containers, or both. Read on, and you may find flowers that, should you decide to plant them, will be the first of their kind ever seen in your neighborhood!

Official USDA-AHS hardiness zones and plant heat-zones are given for each species. Within the given hardiness zone range for a plant, it should not only survive winters, but emerge in a thriving condition. Similarly, within the plant heat-zone range for each plant, it should thrive despite summer heat.

And you probably won't be buying most of the plants on this list by the dozen, but rather a few at a time. Most of these are specimen plants for containers or for focal spots in your landscape. They will usually be for sale in larger pots than bedding plants, and at a slightly higher cost per plant, especially in zones 6 and 7 where shipping costs from producers in the Deep South are relatively high. Most of these are showy plants. Some might even be called spectacular. I recommend you try only as many new ones at a time as you have discrete, separate, outdoor living rooms in your yard. In that way you won't have these garden starlets upstaging each other.

Understand that this is a list of highly personal choices. My list doesn't necessarily reflect the relative popularity of the plant. On the contrary, some of the plants singled out are little known in the South. But I like them, and I hope that you will too. My list doesn't give many cultivar names for the various species, only the ones that are likely to be listed for some time to come. That's where the several lists in chapter 6 will come in handy; they do give cultivar names, and plenty of them, enough to keep you busy ordering plants for several seasons.

Achillea, milfoil, yarrow

(*Achillea millefolium*)

> Hardy perennial; hardiness zones 4–9, heat-zones 9–2
> Mature height: 12 to 19 inches
> Full sun or light shade

Not long ago, this species came only in pink and white colors. Then plant breeders worked their magic and produced several more soft shades in the peach, coral, rose, and crimson range to get the All-America Selections winner, 'Summer Pastels', and

Milfoil (*Achillea millefolium* 'Galaxy Hybrids')

other advanced color mixtures. This yarrow spreads vigorously by roots and forms a mat of ferny, gray-green foliage which may need rigorous trimming every spring. Broad, umbrella-like sprays of tiny flowers come on tall, nearly leafless stems in early summer. If you shear them off when they have turned brown, and feed and water the plants, they should rebloom in late summer. The stems of this yarrow are too soft and wiry to support cut flowers for long. For cutting, plant the yellow-flowered yarrows such as 'Gold Plate'. They are tall and clump-forming.

Allamanda (bush) (*Allamanda schottii*)

Frost-tender tropical shrub; hardiness zone 11, heat-zones 12–7

Mature height in zones 9 and 10: 5 feet

Full sun or light shade

Most everyone in South Florida knows the vining form of allamanda, but the bush type is less common. It is included in this book because it makes an outstanding container plant further north, and can be brought indoors to save for the following year. All summer long, yellow, open-faced blossoms flushed with orange virtually cover the bush, and they wither and drop neatly when spent. During recent years, some growers have offered small blooming plants of allamanda for sale as bedding plants. Allamanda is nearly impervious to summer rains and humidity. Try combining allamanda with purple princess flower (*Tibouchina urvilleana*).

Allamanda, vining type, in Sibley Conservatory, Callaway Gardens

Angel flower (*Angelonia angustifolia*)

Annual in zone 8 and further north; hardiness zones 9–10, heat-zones 10–8

Mature height: 2 feet

Full sun or light shade

This one sneaked up on me. Somehow, in years of visiting flower trials, I never saw it growing. It took a garden tour on the *American Queen* paddlewheeler to introduce me to angelonia, growing at Linden Plantation near Vicksburg, and at Rosalie, an antebellum town house at Natchez. Upon returning home, I pulled out my treasured, dog-eared copy of *An Encyclopedia of Annual and Biennial Garden Plants*, by Charles O. Booth (out of print, unfortunately).

There it was . . . "a showy Mexican species, with smooth, narrow leaves, and long, erect spikes of deep violet flowers." Booth described five other *Angelonia* species as well; I hope that more will appear later in southern gardens. *GrowerTalks* magazine, which featured angelonia in one of its issues, says that thirty species are found in the wild in tropical and subtropical areas. Heat-resistant flowers, especially with blue or purple spikes, are hard to come by. I can't wait to see this one used in containers as a tall accent plant to create a vertical line.

Angel flower (*Angelonia angustifolia*) is often used to add height to sun-washed containers. Shown here (left) with wax begonias.

Angel's trumpet (*Brugsmansia* sp., *Datura* sp.)

> Frost-tender, woody subshrubs; *Brugsmansia*: hardiness zone 11, heat-zone 12–7; *Datura*: hardiness zone 7b, heat-zone 12–7
>
> Mature height: to 10 feet, but 5 feet would be average
>
> Full sun or light shade

A spate of warm winters in hardiness zone 7 has brought many sightings of angel's trumpet. Master gardeners at Spartanburg, South Carolina, tell me the daturas survive winters with no protection in their gardens. It is hard to imagine a showier plant, especially the whites of daturas and the peachy colors of the brugsmansias. Angel's trumpet has large, velvety leaves on thick, sturdy stems that arch out from a central stem three inches or more in diameter. Single-flowered or double "trumpets" hang like bells from the branch tips. Depending on the species and cultivar, they may be white, yellow, orange, creamy pink, or bicolored. The white (rarely pink or yellow) species, *B.* × *candida*, is the most fragrant. In mild-winter areas I've seen brugsmansia plants ten feet tall and even larger in width, but in the Middle South, plants rarely grow more than five feet tall. The somewhat similar daturas grow shorter and wider, and have white flowers. Many gardeners root "starts" from stem cuttings taken from plants with desirable colors and flower forms, or start plants from seeds. Avoid ingesting any plant parts, especially seeds. Do not plant it where children have access to it.

Close-up, Angel's trumpet (*Brugsmansia* sp.)

Balloon flower (*Platycodon grandiflorus*)

Perennial; hardiness zones 4–9, heat-zones 9–1

Mature height: 18 inches for the dwarf cultivar to 30 inches for the standards

Full sun or light shade

Heat and humidity doesn't seem to distress this rugged, easy-care, blue-, white-, or pink-flowered perennial. The blue-flowered cultivar has come back in my garden for several years despite my blundering into the crowns when hoeing weeds. The foliage dies to the ground with the first hard frost and doesn't sprout again until spring is well along. Once you see the unique blossoms of balloon flower, you will always know them at first glance. They are borne singly on branch tips. The corolla inflates like a balloon before splitting into pointed petals and opening wide. You can buy double-flowered cultivars, but there is beauty in the simplicity of the single-flowered types. You will like the steel-blue color of the standard old-fashioned balloon flower. Deadhead the flowers when they have shriveled, and blooming will continue past midsummer. Don't be surprised if your new plants don't bloom the first year; they are typically slow to bloom. As with all hardy perennials, balloon flower may be short-lived in zone 9 and further south.

Balloon flower (*Platycodon grandiflorus*)
PLANT PICS

Banana (ornamental) (*Musa* sp.)

Frost-tender tropical, most species kill to the roots at 45°F; hardiness zone 9 and south, heat-zones 12–7

Height attained in one season: 5 to 10 feet, depending on the cultivar and the heat

Full sun or light shade, protect from wind damage

I can remember from my childhood days in Vicksburg, Mississippi, a banana plant that a homeowner wrapped in several layers of burlap every winter. The burlap must have given sufficient protection because the plant would blossom and set small fruit late

Backlighting brings out the vein patterns on ornamental bananas (*Musa* sp.).

in the summer of the following year. Now, shorter, vividly-colored cultivars of bananas such as blood banana (*M. acuminata* 'Sumatrana') are available to add a dramatic, tropical touch to southern gardens. The long, papery leaves are susceptible to wind damage, thus ornamental bananas are often planted in protected corners or where hedges can cut the force of the wind. In zone 8 and further north, it is a good idea to plant bananas in a twenty- to thirty-gallon container that can be rolled into a garage during the winter to protect them from freezing. Banana plants are hard to find in the Upper South; you may have to order them by mail. Stokes Tropicals has a lengthy list of them available by mail order. Plant Delights Nursery offers *Musa basjoo*, the hardiest species, which has survived most winters in zone 7.

Baptisia, false indigo (*Baptisia alba, B. australis*)

Long-lived perennial, native to the Southeast and prairie
  states; hardiness zones 3–9, heat-zones 9–2
Mature height: to 3 feet
Full sun

Native false white indigo (*Baptisia alba*), roadside near Wilson home

Early every summer, I am cheered by the sight of the asparagus-like spears of white false indigo shooting up through the briars and honeysuckle on roadsides leading to our farm. Once they have penetrated the canopy of brush, the stems branch into open bushes topped with tall, spiraling spikes of white, pealike, leguminous flowers that deliver color for about a month. Several bladderlike seed pods will form on each spike, extending the visual interest. Blue false indigo, *B. australis*, has mid-blue flowers and stays in color somewhat longer than *B. alba*. I have the deep violet-blue cultivar 'Purple Smoke', and especially like its nearly black stems. Although none of the wild indigos are in color all summer, their large, attractive bushes make solid additions to landscapes. Young plants often will not bloom for a full year after transplanting.

The sizeable bushes of wild blue indigo (*Baptisia australis*) make a bold statement in landscapes.

Basil (ornamental) (*Ocimum basilicum*)

Frost-tender perennial, grown as an annual in most zones; hardiness zone 9–10, heat-zones 10–1

Mature height: 18 to 30 inches, depending on the variety

Full sun all day

In my opinion, five of the many species and named varieties of the basils are beautiful enough to qualify as ornamental. I would rank 'African Blue' first, followed by 'Siam Princess', 'Cinnamon', 'Dark Opal', and 'Spicy Globe'. All but 'Spicy Globe' are quite heat- and humidity-resistant. Lacking the time to prune off basil blossoms every week or so, I especially appreciate the fact that 'African Blue' keeps growing and producing despite being loaded down with blossom spikes and seeds. It grows into a large bush, fully thirty inches high by three or four feet across, and attracts flocks of small butterflies, honey bees, and beneficial wasps. If you have typecast the basils as suitable only for herb gardens, you are missing a sure bet. Try them among your flowers, but allow them room to bush out. All the basils are easy to grow in well-drained soil.

Basil (*Ocimum Basilicum* 'African Blue'), in Wilson garden

Beard tongue (*Penstemon* sp.)

Perennial; *P. digitalis*: hardiness zones 2–8, heat-zones 8–1; *P. smallii*: hardiness zones 5–9, heat-zones 9–4; 'Husker Red': hardiness zones 2–8, heat-zones 8–1

Mature height: 18 to 30 inches, depending on the species

Full sun, well-drained soil

It is ironic that some of the most beautiful flowers have the most clinical common names. I love the penstemons for their tall, open sprays of tubular flowers, and the hummingbirds they attract. The lavender-pink native species *P. smallii* survives in the cleared land beneath high-voltage power lines near us, and we can also find the white *P. digitalis* nearby. But my

The white-flowered beard tongue (*Penstemon digitalis*) grows wild in many southern states. It makes a beautiful and long-lived flower for borders.

favorite is the University of Nebraska development, 'Husker Red', winner of the 1996 Perennial Plant of the Year award. I've seen it growing in several foreign countries and over much of North America. It bears a strong resemblance to *P. eriantherus*, a pink-flowered species with purple foliage which is illustrated in the catalog of The Great Plant Company. Some of the exotic penstemons from other countries demand well-drained soil, and can't tolerate our summer rains. Our rugged natives don't seem to mind the occasional summer cloudburst, but they do prefer raised beds filled with sandy soil. Try to replicate their natural habitats and they will live for years, thickening into drifts after a few seasons.

Begonia (wax-leafed) (*Begonia semperflorens*)

> Annual in zones 6 and 7, short-lived perennials further south; hardiness zone 11, further north with protection from evergreen trees; heat-zones 12–1
>
> Mature height: 10 to 24 inches, depending on the variety
>
> Adaptable to full sun or light to moderate shade

I still can't get over the shock of seeing edgings or drifts of wax-leafed begonias flourishing in full sun in the South. Before hybrids such as 'Tausendschoen' were introduced after World War II, begonias needed protection from the southern sun. Their improved tolerance for strong sun and high humidity has greatly increased their popularity in the South. Dozens of varieties are available as small bedding plants or specimen plants in larger pots. Varieties fall into either green- or bronze-leafed types. Usually, the smaller the leaves, and the darker the foliage, the more tolerant the variety is to hot sun. All wax-leafed begonia colors are soft pastels in the pink, rose, coral, crimson, and white palette. Much brighter colors are available in the larger-flowered tuberous-rooted begonia hybrids, but they are suitable only for cool-season growth in the South. Wax-leafed begonias look much better if mulched and not allowed to go dry during droughts. They make marvelous plants for containers and for edging flower beds.

Wax-leafed begonias, Park Seed Co. shaded trials

The recently introduced 'Dragon Wing' begonias are outstanding performers in afternoon shade, especially in containers. Their plants are considerably larger than those of wax begonias.

Black-eyed Susan (*Rudbeckia fulgida, R. hirta*)

Biennial or short-lived perennial, depending on the species and
cultivar; *R. fulgida*: hardiness zones 4–8, heat-zones 8–1; *R. hirta*:
hardiness zones 4–9, heat-zones 9–2

Mature height: dwarf cultivars, 8 to 12 inches; standard-size cultivars:
24 to 36 inches

Full sun or light shade

One of the most widely adapted North American wildflowers is
also widely accepted as a long-blooming perennial for
sunny borders. With their long, showy petals and
prominent, dome-shaped disks, the black-eyed
Susans are one of the core flowers for landscapes. Cultivars from *R. fulgida* var. *sullivantii*, such as 'Goldsturm', are immensely
popular. 'Goldsturm' was selected as the
Perennial Plant of the Year in 1998 by the
Perennial Plant Association. It has broad,
rather heart-shaped leaves and blooms freely
from late summer on. In the wild, *R. fulgida* has
evolved many different plant and blossom sizes and
forms. Some catalogs list selections from these variations under *R. hirta*. In the wild, *R. hirta* blooms a month
earlier than *R. fulgida*, but is not as long-blooming. Also,
R. hirta has long, rough-surfaced, strap-shaped leaves. It
is a short-lived, reseeding perennial, sometimes acting as
a biennial. Plant sizes range from the diminutive
'Becky', at a height of twelve inches, to three feet for
some *R. hirta* selections or hybrids such as the bicolor
'Gloriosa Daisy' and the golden yellow All-America Selections winner, 'Indian Summer'. Botanically speaking, catalogs and tags can't
seem to keep the *Rudbeckia* species straight, but give them a break;
their nomenclature isn't cut and dried with the plant taxonomists
either. By the way, the long-stemmed rudbeckias make first-class
flowers for cutting.

The black-eyed Susans come in many warm colors and blossom forms, and are one of the most dependable classes of perennials for summer color.

Bloodweed, bloodflower (*Asclepias curassavica*)
Butterfly Weed (*A. tuberosa*)

A. curassavica: annual in zone 8 and further
north; hardiness zones 3–9, heat-zones
10–2; *A. tuberosa*: hardiness zones 4–9,
heat-zones 9–1

Mature height: 4 to 5 feet, erect

Full sun or light shade

Bloodweed or bloodflower (*Asclepias curassavica*), Park Seed Co. trials

Butterfly enthusiasts, please note. If you like
to encourage monarch butterflies by offering their
caterpillars a milkweed host plant but hate to see your
butterfly weed (*Asclepias tuberosa*) plants stripped by the
voracious larvae, here is a compromise solution. Plant
this fast-growing milkweed as a sacrificial or trap plant.
The caterpillars will swarm on your plants of bloodweed,
and pressure will be reduced on the slower-growing, less vigorous
plants of butterfly weed. The flower sprays of bloodweed are smaller
than those of butterfly weed, and are a distinctive blood red with
orange or yellow markings. Bloom comes earlier than on butterfly
weed and continues longer. The erect plants are extremely resistant
to heat and humidity, and prefer to be grown on lean, gravelly clay
rather than fertile garden soil.

Blue clock vine (*Thunbergia grandifloria*)

Frost-tender perennial; hardiness zone 11 but
may live over in zones 9 and 10 with
protection, heat-zones 12–1

Mature height: 3 to 5 feet

Full sun

Blue clock vine (*Thunbergia grandiflora*)

As with several other tender species, this
relative of the black-eyed Susan vine can be
grown as an annual in zone 8 and further north.
Its large, velvety, navy-blue blossoms have a contrasting throat. Basically a shrublike plant, it tends to
form short runners and can be pinched into a bush or
trained up a trellis or along stair or porch banisters. Try
it in a container of ten-gallon size; it can outgrow
smaller containers in a single season.

Blue daze (*Evolvulus glomeratus, E. nuttallianus*)

Soft, frost-tender subshrub; hardy to 50°F; hardiness zone 9 and
south, heat-zones 12–7
Mature height: 12 to 18 inches, depending on length of season
Full sun

Ready-made for growing in containers, this spreading plant has
small, gray-green leaves and small, open-faced, blue
flowers, and grows into a mounded form. It doesn't
mind being tucked in among other flowers in
mixed containers and will conform to the
space allotted to it. By midseason the
branches will grow long enough to trail
over the rims of pots or hanging baskets.
Also try massing a few plants for spots of
blue in beds of annuals. I first saw it several
years ago at Victory Garden South at Callaway
Gardens, where it was doing very well in a window box facing west which, in the South, is the
hottest side of the house. But the horticulturist there
had the foresight to mount the window box near a
water faucet so the plants in it could be watered daily.

Blue daze (*Evolvulus glomeratus*) has many small blue
flowers on trailing, blue-
gray plants.

Bougainvillea (*Bougainvillea* sp.)

Tender, climbing vine in zone 10, cascading shrub further north;
hardiness zones 10–11, heat-zones 12–1
Mature height: to 20 feet, depending on freedom from frost
Full sun with protection from wind

Over the years, I suppose I have had more inquiries concerning
bougainvilleas than any other plant. Many gardeners
can't get them to continue blooming after they
have bought them at a garden center or can't
persuade them to rebloom after carrying
them over winter indoors. They are worth
any amount of trouble because their colors
are unmatched for brilliance. If you are
careful about four cultural practices, your
bougainvilleas should deliver complete satis-
faction. First, don't shift your plant up to a

Variegated bougainvillea, U.S. Botanical Garden,
Washington, DC

larger pot the first year. Let it become a bit potbound. Second, feed it monthly during the spring and fall with a fertilizer formulated for flowers, but hold off feeding when it is in flower, and cut back on the frequency of watering. Third, in zones 8 and further north, nip the ends off runners to force the plant to put its energy into flowering. Lastly, when you do shift your plant up to the next larger sized container or hanging basket, don't attempt to straighten out the roots. Set it in the new pot with minimum disturbance to the roots. *The Southern Living Garden Book* lists nearly three dozen bougainvillea cultivars by colors. In garden centers, you will also find many more choices than the common bronze, pink, watermelon, and white colors.

Butterfly bush, buddleia (*Buddleia davidii*)

Woody shrub, rather short-lived unless renewed by annual cutting-back; *B. davidii*: hardiness zones 5–9, heat-zones 9–2; *B. weyeriana*: hardiness zones 6–8, heat-zones 8–6; *B. alternifolia*: hardiness zones 5–9, heat-zones 10–4

Mature height: 6 to 10 feet

Full sun or light shade

No other flower, in my opinion, can top butterfly bush for attracting the big, showy species of butterflies all summer and fall. We have named varieties of various colors in our landscape, and on warm days they are covered with swallowtails of three or four species, and monarch butterflies. Late in the season, gulf fritillaries and clouded sulfurs predominate. While it is true that you can get taller canes and larger bloom spikes by cutting old canes close to the ground in the fall, we don't do it. We'd rather have the softer, more rounded shape of the unpruned bushes. We extended the bloom season on buddlejas by planting the early-blooming fountain buddleja, *B. alternifolia*. Its

Buddleia davidii, a large species of butterfly bush, attracts swarms of these colorful insects, such as this swallowtail.

lavender-pink spikes are shorter and more slender than those of *B. davidii* cultivars, and more fragrant. Give *B. alternifolia* its own bed, away from other shrubs, as it spreads widely and rapidly from roots, especially if mulched. Cut back canes of fountain buddleja right after blooming rather than waiting until fall or winter. We have also tried yellow buddleja, *B. weyeriana*, but it flowers sparsely and its spikes are rather small. It does make a good companion for blue cultivars, however. Our favorite cultivar is the dwarf blue 'Lochinch', a hybrid with genes from *B. fallowiana*.

Caladium (*Caladium bicolor*)

Grown as an annual in zone 10 and further north; heat-zones 12–8

Mature height in fertile soil: 18 to 24 inches in zones 6 and 7, to 36 inches in zone 8 and further south

Light to moderate shade in zones 6 through 8, moderate to heavy shade further south

Caladiums are the signature plant of tree-shaded southern gardens. Although you can purchase the tubers and sprout them yourself in pots filled with peat moss, most gardeners buy potted caladiums that are showing their foliage colors. The leaves are large and usually heart-shaped, either flat or ruffled around the margins. The white and green or white and pink variegations show up best in dark borders, while the pink on green and rose on green bicolors display best in light shade. Some of the newer cultivars have a silvery or bronze cast to their colors. Set the tubers or plants twelve to eighteen inches apart to produce a solid canopy of leaves. Fortify beds for caladiums with plenty of organic matter and feed and water them regularly to avoid marginal scorch on the leaves. Caladium tubers can be left in the ground in hardiness zones 9 and 10, where they grow to such a size that they produce many leaf shoots and very tall stems. Further north, dig caladium tubers just before frost, bring them indoors and let them dry out, and store them in perlite or vermiculite, not touching each other. Storage temperatures should not drop below 60°F. If you are planting large areas and can use twenty-five or more corms of a given cultivar, you can order direct from Caladium World. They sell corms sorted by sizes.

Caladiums in moderate shade, Western Carolina University, Cullowhee, North Carolina

Calla (*Zantedeschia* sp. and hybrids)

Semi-hardy, bulbous perennial, purportedly hardy only to 50°F; hardiness zone 7b with pinestraw mulch, heat-zones 12–8

Mature height: to 18 inches

Full sun or light shade

Callas are occasionally confused with cannas because of the similarity in names, but in no way resemble them. Calla blossoms are borne singly on leafless stems and appear to have been folded into one-sided cones with pointed tips. The stigma is prominent. Depending on the species, the foliage may be dark green or green, spotted with white. For years, the common white calla, *Z. aethiopica*, and the spotted-leaf species, *Z. albomaculata*, were most often seen. Now, however, hybrids with genes from the red or pink species, *Z. rehmannii*, are being widely grown for border accents and cutting. The intergrade colors, some with dark penciling on the margins of the blossoms, are lovely. The plants are spring-blooming, but the foliage stands up well through the summer. Callas die back to the ground in cold weather, but I have seen them survive zone 7b winters with a mulch of pinestraw. Grow them in well-drained soil so that the bulbs won't rot during wet winter weather, or grow in a container filled with a moderately fast-draining soilless mix.

Calla lily with larkspur, Wilson garden

Canna (*Canna × generalis*)

> Perennial, grown from rhizomes that can be left in the ground in zone 7b and further south; hardiness zones 8–11, heat-zones 12–1
>
> Mature height: 2½ to 3 feet for the dwarf cultivars, to 8 feet for standard tall cultivars
>
> Full sun, light shade for the variegated types

See the list of canna cultivars recommended by San Felasco Nurseries on page 127. Many of the best for the Deep South are on it. The Plant Delights Nursery catalog also describes about a dozen cultivars. For small yards the modern dwarf hybrids are preferred. They grow no higher than thirty to thirty-six inches and are used mostly as background plants for brightly colored annuals that can hold their own with the bold foliage and forthright blossom colors of cannas. You will also see cannas planted on low islands in ponds and in wet soil along streamsides. Being denizens of marshes originally, they can live in soil that is nearly, but not quite, covered with water. Of the canna cultivars, my favorite is the AAS (All-America Selections) award winning 'Tropical Rose'. Its dwarf habit

Canna × generalis 'Linage' is one of the better cultivars with spotted flowers.

The new short cannas such as the All-America Selections award winning 'Tropical Rose' are favored for small gardens and containers.

and soft pink blossoms make it easy to fit into mixed borders. I also like the Bengal Tiger, 'Pretoria', and 'Tropicana' for their flamboyant striped leaves and long, dark bloom stalks. Though it is a bit risky, in zone 6 you can plant cannas in raised beds and mulch them with pinestraw to overwinter them. It usually, but not always, works. Good-hearted neighbors may offer you rhizomes from their good old cannas, but if you can tactfully refuse them, you'll be better off with the new dwarf kinds with pleasing colors than with the old, tall, passalong, heirloom plants with their brash blossoms.

Cassia, senna (*Senna* spp.)

Semi-hardy shrub, may overwinter in zone 8b and further south, although both *S. corymbosa* and *S. alata* purportedly decline at 41–45°F; heat-zones 12–7

Mature height: 6 to 10 feet, equally as wide

Full sun

My introduction to the cassias came forty years ago when I tried to buy quantities of seeds of candleflower (*S. alata*) for selling in seed packets. Since they had to be hand-harvested and seed yields were low, that idea never got off the ground. I still love candleflower, despite its stiffish plants, coarse foliage, and very late bloom, because its massive candelabras of waxy, yellow flowers create such a visual impact in landscapes. Now that I've traveled more and have seen the reliance that gardeners in zone 8 and further south place on summer cassia (*S. corymbosa*), it is my new favorite. Its bushes grow big, up to ten feet tall and equally wide, and are covered with large, open sprays of light yellow flowers that keep coming and coming. Such an abundance of spent blossoms fall to the ground that it looks like a yellow carpet. Several more species of senna remain under the botanical name *Cassia* and are available in zones 9 and 10, including some that grow to the size of small trees.

Rainbow shower
(*Cassia javanica*)

PLANT PICS

Castiron plant, barroom plant, stovetop plant

(*Aspidistra* sp.)

Semi-hardy foliage plant, certain species may overwinter in zone 8,
　　but the tops will freeze during severe winters; heat-zones 12–1
Mature height: 18 to 30 inches, depending on the species
Moderate to fairly dense shade

Plant Delights Nursery offers several aspidistras increased from plants collected in China. They include some of the most shade-tolerant species of any genus. Some resemble the traditional castiron plant, with long, ribbed, dark green leaves with long petioles, while others have narrow leaves speckled with yellow. One heirloom selection, 'Akebono', has a white stripe down the length of the leaf. Most of the aspidistras act as evergreens in zone 8b and further south. If the tops are damaged by freezing, they can be sheared back in the spring to stimulate pristine new spring growth. These are virtually trouble-free plants that will grow under conditions too daunting for other species. You would never expect a song to be written about a plant like aspidistra but the Brits have one, "The Grandest Aspidistra in the World!"

Cat's whiskers (*Orthosiphon stamineus*)

Frost-tender perennial, grown as an annual
　　zone 10 and further north; heat-zones
　　12–8
Mature height: 3 to 4 feet
Full sun to light shade

I fell for this plant, hook, line, and sinker when I first saw it at Leu Gardens in Orlando, Florida. They had the white-flowered variety, and since then I've seen a medium-blue variety as well. I'm partial to the white because the blossoms display so well against the dark green foliage. The tight sprays are about four inches long and cone- shaped, with the lower blossoms opening first. From the blossoms extend long, up-curving stamens that look for all the world like kitty whiskers. I found cat's whiskers easy to grow in my zone 7 garden. The plants bloomed all summer long, with new spikes coming on to replace the spent flowers. I've begun to see plants for sale in local garden centers; apparently, people other than cat fanciers share my affection for cat's whiskers.

The tropical cat's whiskers (*Orthosiphon* sp.) comes in lavender-blue as well as pure white.

Celosia (*Celosia argentia*)

Annual, grown from seedlings or from direct-seeding in the garden;
  may overwinter in hardiness zones 10–11, heat-zones 12–1
Mature height: 14 to 36 inches, depending on the variety
Full sun, excellent container plants

Dwarf cockscomb 'Amigo Mahogany Red'

The celosias are not exclusively southern flowers, but are grown over much of the USA, and are prized for their resistance to heat and moderate drought-tolerance. The tall varieties of both plume celosia and the crested celosia called "cockscomb" are so vigorous that they will stay in color for two or three months. The dwarf varieties are so short that they tend either to become disfigured from splashed soil, or burned out from the heat by August. They have such large flower spikes, or cockscombs, for the size of the plants that they can't generate new growth while fighting off the effects of the hot sun. All the celosias are good for cutting, especially the crested types with comparatively small heads on long stems. Wheat celosia, a selection with grasslike leaves, was recently introduced. It has slender, bicolored flower spikes that are also good for cutting. All types can be used in arrangements, fresh or dried. If you start celosias from plants, buy the youngest ones you can find. At near full bloom stage, celosias are susceptible to transplant shock no matter how carefully you set them out. The slick, black seeds of celosia sprout quickly in warm, moist soil in the garden and the seedlings will transplant easily and surely when small. Plant the pink shades with blue salvia; they bloom at about the same time.

Coleus (sun tolerant) (*Solenostemon scutellariodes*)

Annual in zones 9 and further north, short-lived in perennial zone 10;
  hardiness zones 10–11, heat-zones 12–1
Mature height: to 3 or 4 feet
Light to moderate shade in zone 8 and further south, full sun or light
  shade further north

Recently given a new botanical name, coleus is winning a new place in landscapes, thanks to the introduction of several sun-tolerant, vegetatively-propagated cultivars. They are sold in series of colors under such names as 'Sunlover', 'Solar', 'Ducksfoot', and 'Hurricane'. The latter three series were developed by Hatchett Creek Farms in

Sun-tolerant coleus. Here are just a few of the available cultivars: L to R, 'Alabama,' 'Flair,' and 'Cranberry'. Photographed in Charleston, SC

Gainesville, Florida. The plants of the sun-tolerant kinds differ from the traditional shade plant coleus in that they are generally larger-leafed, denser-growing, and much slower to flower. While they can tolerate full sun, they are less prone to looking wilted if grown in afternoon shade or high shade from trees and watered three times weekly during dry spells. Their colors are less likely to look bleached in the shade. Most large-leafed cultivars will grow into big bushes by the season's end, but the little-leafed 'Trailing Red' puts its energy into spreading rather than growing tall. Here are just a few other available cultivars: 'Alabama Sunrise', 'Cranberry', 'Flair', 'Plum Parfait', and 'Burgundy Sun'. Some retailers offer as many as a dozen color variegations. Most cultivars are variegated or bordered with contrasting colors, with base colors ranging from chartreuse to pink and deep burgundy. I like to see these cultivars grown as individual plants in three-gallon pots, or massed in beds. The plants are so flamboyant that they can jangle the serenity of a bed of mixed annuals.

Coneflower *(Echinacea purpurea, E. paradoxa, Ratibida sp.)*

Perennial, long-lived in zones 6 and 7; *E. purpurea*: hardiness zones 3–9, heat-zones 9–1; *R. columnifera*: hardiness zones 3–10, heat-zones 10–1

Mature height: 2 to 4 feet, depending on the species

Full sun or light shade

Cultivars from these two hardy perennial native North American *Echinacea* species make up most of the catalog and plant offerings in coneflowers. There are several other wild echinaceas but some of them are federally protected. Protection is needed because of heavy and widespread harvesting of various wild *Echinacea* species for medicinal purposes. The *Echinacea* species have long-stemmed, long-lasting, daisylike blossoms with prominent dark disks, but the colors are different. In *E. purpurea* you can find cultivars with purple, pink, rose, and white ray petals. Paradoxically, the blossoms of *E. paradoxa* resemble black-eyed

Pink-flowered selection of purple coneflower (*Echinacea purpurea*)

Left: **Mexican hat (*Ratibida columnifera*). Mature plant in Wilson garden**
Right: **Gray-head coneflower (*Ratibida pinnata*)**

Susans in color and form. The perennial ratibidas only superficially resemble the echinaceas. *Ratibida* cultivars have either yellow or, in the Mexican-hat variation, yellow-mahogany bicolored blossoms, but their lacy leaves are so ferny and silvery blue that there is no mistaking their identity. Their disks are slender and protuberant. All the coneflowers make good flowers for cutting, and all are visited by many species of butterflies. All can endure dry soil and high temperatures, but suffer from excessive rain and soggy soil. All benefit from being cut back, fed, and watered after the first flush of bloom, and all will flower again.

Confederate rose (*Hibiscus mutabilis*)

> Woody perennial, freezes partway back or to the ground, but usually regrows; official hardiness zone rating indicates it declines at temperatures less than 55°F, heat-zones 12–8
>
> Mature height: 10 to 15 feet, depending on soil fertility and the age of the clump
>
> Full sun or light shade

Someone used a great deal of poetic license in naming this one. It doesn't remotely resemble a rose, and it hails from South China. Blooming is triggered by the lengthening of nights, and in zone 7 you will see no color until along in October. If frost comes early, it can cut down the top growth before many blooms open. However, in an extended warm fall, you can enjoy the sight of hundreds of huge

Confederate rose (*Hibiscus mutabilis*) in Wilson garden.
JANE WILSON

blooms opening at the tips of tall canes, even after a light frost. In zone 8 and further south, blooming can continue for a month or more. The plants can reach ten to fifteen feet in height in rich soil, and have dozens of canes. Our plants are the pink, fully double type. In the nearby town of Greenwood I've seen a white-flowered type, whose flowers turn deep rose with age. I understand that a crimson variety is known, but I haven't seen one. We occasionally lose our plants during hard winters, and always keep stem cuttings rooting in water. They look like sticks of green wood but root readily. New bushes will grow quickly from rooted cuttings and bloom the same growing season.

Coral bells, heuchera, American alumroot (*Heuchera* spp.)

Perennial; hardiness zones 4–8, heat-zones 8–1
Mature height: 12 to 24 inches, depending on the cultivar and site
Light to moderate shade

Most northern gardeners know coral bells as a good performer in either full sun or light shade. But in the South, the coral bells perform better with more protection from the sun. The purple-leafed cultivars seem to have the most tolerance for sunny situations. Hummingbirds take nectar from the tiny blossoms, but watching them work at it, the gain hardly seems worth the pain. Coral bells have changed greatly during the past two decades. Crosses between species (interspecific) have produced cultivars with silvery, bronze, and purple foliage, sometimes mottled or accented with contrasting colors. And the colors of the tiny, bell-shaped blossoms now include white and several shades of pink, coral, and red. With this achievement, breeders boosted coral bells into the top tier of perennials, and 'Palace Purple' was named the 1991 Perennial Plant of the Year. Now, with the creation of intergeneric crosses between the genus *Heuchera* and *Tiarella* (foamflower), the choice of flower and foliage colors is even greater. Foamflower, a native woodland wildflower, brings good shade tolerance to these new crosses, referred to as heucherellas or foamy bells.

Coral vine, rosa de montana, confederate vine

(*Antigonon leptopus*)

Tropical vine; hardiness zones 9–11, heat-zones 12–7, grown as an
annual in the Midsouth

Mature height: 10 to 15 feet, more in the Deep South

Full sun

I've been fond of this coral-pink–flowered vine ever since seeing
it used to screen porches in South Texas years ago. We featured it in

a *Victory Garden* show taped at Callaway
Gardens which should have whetted
interest across the South. It can become a
nuisance in zones 9 and 10, spreading
high and wide and coming up everywhere
from seeds. Down in the Yucatan, I saw it
clinging to and half-smothering all the
shrubs in the yard of a hacienda where we
stayed. However, it freezes out in zone 8
and further north, and is easy to control as
an annual. Coral vine bears numerous
erect, loose spikes of small, coral-pink

**Towering over this
garden of mixed wild-
flowers and showy
perennials is coral vine
(*Antigonon leptopus*).
Callaway Gardens**

flowers all summer long. I've seen red and white varieties but don't believe they are in commerce. It may
hold the record for the most common names given any
flower. *Hortus Third* lists ten of them! (Hold the phone;
I just learned that Professor Michael Dirr's research on
the European water lily turned up the staggering totals of 15 English
common names for it, plus 46 French, 105 German, and 81 Dutch.)

Coreopsis (*Coreopsis grandiflora, C. verticillata*)

Biennial or short-lived perennial; hardiness zones 4–9, heat-zones 9–1

Mature height: 16 to 24 inches

Full sun or light shade

Few other flowers can bring such sunny cheer to gardens as the
yellow-gold summer-flowering coreopsis cultivars. (There is a rose-
colored species but it isn't strongly heat resistant.) Originally native
American wildflowers, they have been extensively selected for larger
flowers, extended season of bloom, and more compact plants. *C.
grandiflora*, sometimes called "lance-leafed coreopsis," can be had in
fully double, semi-double, and single-flowered varieties, with heights
ranging from nine inches to two feet depending on the variety. Most

Prairie coreopsis (*Coreopsis tinctoria*) blooms early on plants that grow from seeds dropped the previous summer. Many blossoms are variegated.

are short-lived perennials which drop seeds and produce loads of volunteers. The rangier varieties are more vigorous and are used in wildflower seed mixtures. Cultivars of the threadleaf coreopsis, *C. verticillata*, are longer-lived than their sister species, and have smaller flowers of a lighter yellow tint. The cultivar 'Moonbeam' is wildly popular and was honored with a Perennial Plant of the Year award several years ago. However, I agree with University of Georgia Professor Allan Armitrage's contention that 'Zagreb' is the toughest and best-performing cultivar of the species. All coreopsis grow best in well-drained soil and can withstand drought fairly well.

Cosmos (*Cosmos bipinnatus, C. sulphureus*)

Annual, can be grown from seedlings or by direct-seeding; heat-zones

12–1

Mature height: 24 to 36 inches

Full sun

Unfortunately, the cosmos species with the most colors— white, pink, rose, and cherry-red—and many fancy petal forms is only moderately heat-resistant. It is the fern-leafed *C. bipinnatus*. On the other hand, it would be hard to find a more durable summer flower than the yellow, gold, and bronze-red *C. sulphureus*. It has wiry stems and rough leaves that look distressingly like giant ragweed, so do be careful when weeding a bed of it. Both are highway flowers, widely planted in southern interstate freeway medians, where they are direct-seeded in midsummer. Summer rains bring up the seeds and blossoms can begin showing in as little as forty-five days after germination. The blossoms are large and mostly single on *C. bipinnatus*, smaller and semi-double to double on *C. sulphureus*. Both species are great butterfly flowers, and finches will come in for the dry seeds

Cosmos (*Cosmos sulphureus* 'Ladybird Mixed Colors') at Park Seed Co. trials in the fall. I only hope the pretty little things learn to take off verti-cally so they don't challenge eighteen-wheelers for the right-of-way.

Crinum, hardy crinum lily (*Crinum* spp.)

Bulbous perennial, with some species hardy through zone 7;
C. *latifolium*: hardiness zones 10–11, heat-zones 12–7; *C. asiaticum*
and *C. jagus*: hardiness zones 8–11, heat-zones 12–8
Mature height of flower cluster: 24 to 36 inches
Full sun or light shade

The crinums belong to a large and confusing genus of bulbous plants, with so few obvious differences between some species that common names such as "milk and wine" are used interchangeably by home gardeners. *Garden Bulbs for the South* by Scott Ogden holds that milk and wine lilies, botanically speaking, are *C.* × *herbertii*, while John Bryan's book, *Bulbs*, identifies them as *C. latifolium*. *Hortus Third* splits it a little finer by calling milk and wine lily *C. latifolium* 'Zeylanicum'. Whatever the botanical designation, milk and wine lily has out-facing white blossoms with red-purple stripes that will remind you of amaryllis. Some red and white or cream crinums that belong to the hybrid *C.* × *powellii* are sometimes sold as milk and wine lilies to take advantage of the well-known common name. In the Middle and Upper South, the important thing to look for in crinums is winter hardiness. In well-drained soil, the *C. latifolium* and *C. powellii* culti-vars are hardy through zone 7, and into zone 6 with a deep but loose mulch. The crinums form very large bulbs that shoot up long, smooth, straplike leaves, and thick flowering stems to three feet in height. In zones 8 and 9, such tender species as *C. asiaticum* and *C. jagus* are more popular. Crinum bulbs should be left undisturbed except when taking offsets for transplanting else-where. Summer-bulb mail-order specialists such as Stokes Tropicals offer a large selection of crinum cultivars, as does Old House Gardens, specialists in old-timey bulbous flowers. Before investing heavily in crinum bulbs, ask the nearest botanical garden which species are hardy for them, and plant accordingly.

"Milk and wine" crinum lily, Wilson garden

Cupflower (*Nierembergia hippomanica, N. repens*)

    Short-lived perennial; hardiness zones 7–10, heat-zones 10–7

    Mature size: 4 to 6 inches high by 12 inches across

    Full sun

In the 1960s, I saw the spreading 'Purple Robe' variety of cupflower blooming merrily in the midsummer heat of West Tennessee. So I shouldn't have been surprised to see how well the All-America Selections award winner, 'Mont Blanc', performed in the South. However, it is such a diminutive plant that you wouldn't expect it to stand up to heat and humidity. It does in zone 8 and further north, but performs better during the winter further south. The blue-flowered variety grows about twice as large as the pure white 'Mont Blanc'. My 'Mont Blanc' plants have lived through two mild winters, but I must say that the young plants I added to my mulched edging have produced many more flowers than the elderly survivors. Both varieties are frequently used in hanging baskets where they can tumble over the rim.

Closeup, young plant of *Nierembergia* 'Mont Blanc', Wilson home

Dahlberg daisy, golden fleece (*Thymophylla tenuiloba*, formerly *Dyssodia tenuiloba*)

    Short-lived perennial, usually grown as an annual; heat-zones 12–1

    Mature size: 8 inches high by 12 to 16 inches across

    Full sun, sandy soil or raised beds

At a state meeting of Master Gardeners in Phoenix, Arizona, I was amazed to see edgings of this little, fern-leafed flower blooming in temperatures well above 100°F. Not surprisingly, it is a native of the desert Southwest. Its heat resistance adapts this species to hardiness zones six, seven, and eight, but the summer humidity further south can do it in. Consequently, it is used as a winter annual along the Gulf Coast. The tiny leaves and wiry but lax stems of Dahlberg daisy recover quickly from beating rains, and the show of small, yellow, double daisy blossoms goes on all summer. You may have

Dahlberg daisy (*Thymophylla tenuiloba*)

seen it used in dish gardens (mixed species planted together in containers) and hanging baskets and wondered what it was. Now you know.

Daylily (*Hemerocallis* cultivars)

Hardy perennial; the deciduous types freeze to the ground; in the
Deep South, the ever-green types stay green during the winter;
most cultivars: hardiness zones 3–10, heat-zones 12–1
Mature height: 14 inches to 5 feet, depending on the cultivar
Full sun

In North America, daylilies are without question the number one hardy perennial in popularity. Breeding daylilies commenced in Europe more than a century ago and continues worldwide. Both commercial companies and individual hobbyists are involved. Daylily breeders were tinkering with producing triploid cultivars before gene linkage was fully understood. Yet, by tripling the chromosome number in cell nuclei and with a lot of luck, many extraordinarily beautiful cultivars have been produced. Most breeders settle for working with diploid crosses, which are simpler and less likely to produce bizarre results. Out of this blizzard of activity have come literally thousands of cultivars, most of which have disappeared from the trade. Desirable modern hybrids offer high bud count; extended bloom span; large, fancy blossoms, perhaps fringed or wavy; unusual colors; and short plants. The fun way to shop for daylilies is to drive to your nearest daylily nursery (after phoning ahead to ascertain peak bloom time), pick out the cultivars you like, dig them, put them in bags, and take them home for planting posthaste. Some of the recent winners of Hemerocallis Society awards will be priced sky-high, as indeed they should be. Most of us let the collectors have first run at them and wait a few years until the price has dropped to affordable levels. No single daylily cultivar will bloom all summer long, but by choosing early, midseason, and late varieties, you can have successive bloom from May or June through July or August, depending on your climate. If your summer proves cool, color may continue a month longer. By the way, deer and rabbits *love* daylilies, so if you live where they are a problem, get a yappy dog.

Typical modern daylily cultivar

Elephant ears, taro (*Alocasia, Colocasia* sp.)

> Aquatic, tropical perennials, with some species hardy
> through zone 7b; official hardiness zones 9–11,
> heat-zones 12–4
> Mature height: 3 to 10 feet
> Full sun to light shade

Elephant ear,
variegated
form
(*Alocasia
macrorrhiza*)
PLANT PICS

I have watched patches of taro, *Colocasia esculenta*, growing in yards near my home, fully expecting them to freeze out come winter. But they come back year after year with no protection, because they were grown next to a south-facing wall. And I have seen plants of the elegant, bicolored, fancy-leafed cultivars of 'African Mask', *A. amazonica*, thriving and coming back in courtyard gardens near the battery in Charleston, South Carolina. But those are exceptions, and the other shoe will drop some frigid winter day. Far more of these big, bold plants are grown in zones 9 and 10 where they usually survive winters out-of-doors, even if partially frozen back during drastic drops in temperature. In zones 6 and 7, tubers can be dug and brought indoors, stored dry, and replanted the next spring. In zones 7 and 8, they can be mulched with pinestraw before the first heavy freeze, after trimming off the tops. Even though these are aquatic species in the wild, they will grow quite well in fertile garden soil if watered frequently and fed once a month. For elephant ears as big as Dumbo's, grow the giant upright elephant ear *A. macorrhizos*. For dramatic effect plant the green on purple-black *C. esculenta* 'Antiquorum', 'Illustris', or 'Black Magic'.

Eustoma, lisianthus, Texas bluebell (*Eustoma grandiflorum*)

> Short-lived perennial, usually grown as an annual; hardiness zones
> 8–10, heat-zones 12–1
> Mature height: to 18 inches. Dwarf varieties can mature at 8 to 10
> inches
> Full sun or light shade

In just a few years this Texas native wildflower has risen to the status of a major flower for southern landscapes and for cutting. Breeders have attempted to improve it by dwarfing the plants, but even at a height of only twelve inches, the dwarf varieties tend to

Dwarf variety of Texas bluebells (*Eustoma grandiflora*) at Park Seed Co. trials

flop. I prefer the elegant tall varieties with sprays of blossoms atop eighteen-inch stems, even if they have to be staked and tied. They are worth the trouble. The smooth foliage of eustoma is an attractive dusty blue-green, and it looks good in arrangements. I've kept eustoma blossoms in a vase for ten days with little deterioration. The single-flowered varieties look a bit like open-faced tulips, but the double-flowered blossoms more closely resemble large portulaca flowers. Few home gardeners are willing to endure the four-month seed-to-flower time frame for eustoma, preferring instead to purchase plants. Try 'Heidi' or 'Double Eagle' hybrids for double flowers in white, pink, blue, and purple shades. Eustoma is very heat-resistant if grown on well-drained soils. I've seen fields of it in its native Texas habitat and know that it can tolerate dry soil fairly well.

Evening primrose, sundrops (*Oenothera* sp.)

Biennial or hardy perennial, depending on the species; *O. speciosa* and
   O. macrocarpa: hardiness zones 5–8, heat-zones 8–3; *O. fruticosa*:
   hardiness zones 4–8, heat-zones 8–1
Mature height: 14 inches to 5 feet
   Full sun or light shade

This huge genus includes many North American native species which have gravitated into home gardens. Included are the species that bloom in the evening and close the following morning, and the day-blooming species such as sundrops. I've grown four of the species in my wildflower meadow and like three of them—Missouri primrose (*O. macrocarpa*); one called "sundrops" locally (*O. fruiticosa*); showy primrose (*O. speciosa*); and one of the evening-blooming species, *O. biennis*. Missouri primrose has to be my favorite because of its huge, clear yellow blossoms to four inches across and its reddish, spotted, and winged calyxes. It grows to about twelve inches high and sprawls a bit. Its blossoms stay open all day. Sundrops run it a close second. It is also day-

Showy primrose (*Oenothera speciosa*), Ridgeway home garden, Donalds, SC

blooming, with waxy yellow flowers and erect plants around eighteen inches tall. Showy primrose is a lovable scamp of a groundcover. In one season a single plant in a six-inch pot rambled to cover a circle six feet across in my garden. Its medium-sized, light pink blossoms seem to smother the prostrate plants during early summer, and intermittently thereafter. The one primrose I won't invite again into my garden is the huge, invasive, evening primrose *O. biennis.* When it appeared to have the potential for taking over my entire yard, I eradicated it. The western species *O. hookeri* has larger flowers and more compact plants; it is welcome in my garden any time. None of the oenotheras bloom all summer long but are well worth planting among your showy perennials native to other countries.

Missouri primrose (*Oenothera macrocarpa*), Park Seed Co. trials

Fan flower (*Scaevola aemula*)

Usually grown as an annual; declines at 41°F, heat-zones 12–1

Mature size: 6 inches high, 18 inches in diameter

Full sun, light shade in the Deep South

Fan flower made its debut as a hanging-basket flower a decade or so ago, and few people thought it would survive southern summers. It grows quite well through zone 8 but is usually reserved for winter color further south. The plants are lax and spreading, with odd, one-sided, lavender-blue or purple blossoms spangled down the length of the branches. It can grow in ground beds but prefers the good drainage of sandy soil in raised beds or the moderately fast drainage of containers. On heavy soil the matted foliage of fan flower traps moisture, which invites foliage diseases. To encourage

Fanflower (*Scaevola aemula*), is valued for containers and hanging baskets.

Close up, the blue blossoms of fanflower (*Scaevola aemula*) show how it got its common name.

fan flower to continue blooming, you will need to feed and water it more than is customary for garden or container flowers. It is available in medium blue, lavender-blue, white, and purple colors.

Ferns (many genera and species)

Most native species of ferns are hardy in all southern zones. Some exotic species are tropical in origin and won't survive north of zone 9.

Mature height: ranges from very short, such as ebony spleenwort, to the tall and erect cinnamon fern

Moderate shade to dense shade—the former is preferred

Bracken fern grows among spears of scouring rush in a low, moist woodland.

In shaded southern gardens, the winter-hardy ferns take over after the spring-blooming, forest floor wildflowers have faded into the wallpaper. Many of the hardy ferns freeze to the ground during the winter and send up new fronds in late spring. For tall plants, set back some distance from paths, I like royal fern and ostrich fern. For medium-height plants, I like Christmas fern and southern maidenhair. But I suppose, of all the ferns, I like the Japanese painted fern best. *Athyrium niponicum* 'Pictum' has tricolored foliage with a silvery cast to the colors. It freezes back in the Middle and Upper South but is winter-hardy. It prefers light shade.

In gardens in the Deep South, the evergreen ferns will flourish where shade is too dense for most flowering plants. In moderate shade, the glossy-leafed holly ferns shine in zone eight and further south, and may survive winters in zone 7 if given protection from drying winds. A fern specialist gave me a hint about growing them that may prove useful to you. Under trees, where root competition can dry out ferns, sink a pad of bricks into the soil and plant the ferns around it. Moisture will collect beneath the bricks and sustain the ferns longer.

Firebush (*Hamelia patens*)

A frost-tender subshrub hardy in zone 9 and further south, grown like tropical hibiscus further north; heat-zones 12–7

Mature height: 4 to 5 feet in zone 9, taller in warmer climates

Full sun

A Florida native perennial, firebush is also appearing in gardens further north where it is brought indoors for winter protection. In zone eight, against a south-facing wall, it will grow into a subshrub four feet tall in one season. It lights up landscapes with large spikes of closely packed, orange-red, tubular flowers from midsummer on. Hummingbirds and butterflies will flock to it for nectar, and wild birds for the dark berries that form in the fall. If I had to chose one "in your face" flower for zones 8 and further north, firebush would be it. Planted amongst the generally mannerly colors of typical midsouthern borders, it looks like a showgirl at a Girl Scout cookie meeting. In zones 8 and further north tender plants such as firebush are the best argument for installing fluorescent light fixtures or metal halide lamps that can be used to root and carry cuttings through the winter for spring planting.

Firebush at Riverbanks Zoo & Botanical Garden, Columbia, SC

Firecracker vine, candy corn vine (*Manettia cordifolia,*
M. luteorubra)

> Semi-hardy vines, will survive most winters in zone 7b, officially
>   decline at 45°F; heat-zones 12–1
> Mature height: to 5 feet, taller in the Deep South
> Full sun to light shade

Firecracker vine came to me without a name some five years ago, and I dubbed it "hummingbird vine" for the number of hummers that visited its bright red, tubular flowers. Not until a visit to southern California some time later where I saw firecracker vine plants for sale in a nursery, labeled by their botanical name *Manettia*, did I have a clue as to where to look for a description of the species. I searched through my good old *Hortus Third* and found that it described all the manettias in commerce. (Not until the day when we can tap into a comprehensive and up-to-date database on all species of flowering plants can we avoid such circuitous searches for plant names.)

My firecracker vine, which I tie to the post of a plantation bell, has survived winter temperatures of near 0°F. It dies to the ground but sprouts in late spring from tubers. The foliage is small, narrow, pointed, glistening dark green, and very handsome, making it a good plant for large hanging baskets. My vine has endured long periods of dry weather; I would rate it highly for desirability. Candy corn vine, a sister species, is already being promoted for containers despite its not being as free-flowering as firecracker vine. The catchy name accurately describes the shiny orange flowers with yellow tips. I haven't tested candy corn vine for winter hardiness, but with a deep mulch of pinestraw, it might come through winters in the Midsouth. Note: don't confuse *M. cordifolia* with *Ipmoea lobata* (formerly *Mina lobata*) which also is known as firecracker vine.

Firetails, strawberry firetails (*Acalypha pendula*)

Tender perennial, grown as an annual zone 8 and further north; hardiness zones 9–11, heat-zones 10–7

Spreading plant with pendulous branches; height: about 1 foot, spread: 2 feet

Full sun

Hanging basket of strawberry firetails (*Acalypha pendula*) at Weidner's Greenhouses, Encinitas, California

You will see this little flower being sold in hanging baskets across the South. Its numerous tassels look like short, furry pieces of bright red chenille, which accounts for the picturesque name. With minimal feeding and regular watering, firetails will stay in color from mid-summer until frost. A friend in Augusta, Georgia, grows firetails as a bedding plant and mulches the plants with pine bark. They make nicely rounded and mounded plants, but most of the color is around the perimeter where the branch tips touch the mulch. I like their looks better when they are in baskets where the "firetails" can hang down. Display firetails as a conversation piece near your patio where friends gather.

Flowering ginger, ginger lily (*Hedychium* sp., *Curcuma* sp.)

Rhizomatous species with a few species hardy in zone 7; official hardiness zone range on *H. coronarium* is 9–10, heat-zone 10–7. *Curcuma* spp. are not hardy; their heat-zone range is 12–9

Mature height of the flowering gingers: 4 to 5 feet, taller where summers are very long and hot. The Curcumas are much shorter, averaging 24 to 30 inches.

Light to moderate shade

I have grown only the common white flowering ginger (*H. coronarium*), and even though it has survived some pretty harsh winters, I feel it is because I grow it next to the foundation of the west-facing wall of a building. Thus protected, the rhizomes live over reliably in the Piedmont. Yet Tony Avent's bodacious Plant Delights catalog gives me hope that I can also grow several of the yellow, orange, and red species. I love the fragrance of the flowering gingers, and despite their late blooming habit and tall growth, I feel that they deserve a place among southern garden favorites. In the Middle and Upper South, few retailers offer plants or rhizomes of the flowering gingers, but mail-order sources can fill your needs. Just be sure you check the height of the species as well as its winter hardiness. Heights can range from two to eight feet, depending on the species. Several tender species of pine cone ginger (*Curcuma* sp.) are showing up in dish gardens of mixed kinds shipped from the Deep South. Plant Delights Nursery offers three cultivars which are hardy in zone 7b.

**Flowering ginger
(*Hedychium coronarium*)**
PLANT PICS

Gaura (*Gaura lindheimeri, G. coccinea*)

Perennial; hardiness zones 6–9, heat-zones 9–1

Height: 3 to 4 feet

Full sun

The white, day-blooming species of gaura, G. *lindheimeri*, jumped into international prominence with the introduction of larger-flowered cultivars such as 'Whirling Butterflies' and additional colors such as 'Siskiyou Pink'. I first saw G. *lindheimeri* growing wild in East Texas, and during recent years have seen it in botanical and private gardens in several foreign countries. It bears asymmetrical blossoms with thin petals on many tall, slender stems. The slightest breeze will set the stems and blossoms in motion. You will like the neat plants; they slowly thicken into sizable clumps but don't overrun nearby flowers. White gaura will adapt to many soil types, but prefers soils with a clay content. In

Guara lindheimeri 'Siskiyou Pink' was selected from the native white species.

Wildflowers of Texas, Geyata Ajilvsgi describes the evening-opening, fragrant G. *coccinea*, or scarlet gaura. It only faintly resembles white gaura. Its leaves hug the tall stems closely, and its blossoms look like little orchids. The "scarlet" description is optimistic—actually, the blossoms open white and turn pink with age. Grow G. *coccinea* on sandy soil or in raised beds of clay soil for good drainage.

These young plants of globe amaranth (*Gomphrena Haageana* 'Strawberry Fields') will set many blossoms and grow to a height of eighteen inches or so.

The color range in *Gomphrena globosa* is greater than in *G. haageana*.

Globe amaranth *(Gomphrena globosa, G. haageana)*

Annual; heat-zones 12–1

Mature size: 2 feet high, 2½ feet across

Full sun

Generations of southerners have grown this leading everlasting flower for fresh and dried bouquets. It blooms through all kinds of weather and will tolerate fairly long dry spells. Seed breeders produced a couple of dwarf selections many years ago, 'Buddy' and 'Cissy', in pink and purple colors, but did little with the tall types until they selected 'Strawberry Fields' from *G. haageana*. It has dark red, cloverlike blossoms on erect, nearly leafless stems. Breeders also selected a nice lavender color to add to the existing pink, white, and purple shades of *G. globosa*. For winter bouquets, harvest the flowers when they are only half open or they will shatter upon drying. Neither species is particular about soil or watering, but need to be protected if gray and black blister beetles begin eating the foliage; they can strip plants in only a few days.

The dwarf *G. globosa* 'Cissy' in Park Seed Co. trials

Glory bush, princess flower *(Tibouchina urvilleana)*

Tender tropical shrub or small tree, may overwinter in zones 9 and 10; heat-zones 12–3

Mature height: 4 feet where grown as an annual, much taller in the Deep South

Full sun

Garden centers in zones 6, 7, and 8 sell out of this exotic tropical as soon as they display it. Gardeners are taken by its large, deep-purple blossoms, and the reddish cast to the velvety leaves. The plants are leggy and rather awkward, and are often interplanted with sennas for golden contrast. *The Victory Garden* showed this combination growing at Bellingrath Gardens near Mobile, Alabama, and got much positive feedback. You can encourage flower formation by nipping off the longest stems. Taking out just the tip buds is called "pinching," and if done carefully will delay the bloom date only a couple of weeks while forcing the formation of more branches. The big show of bloom color will come in early summer,

Glory bush (*Tibouchina Urvilleana*) PLANT PICS

but with pruning and feeding, the plants will bloom intermittently until fall. Between bursts of bloom, the multicolored foliage saves glory bush from mediocrity. In the Midsouth and Upper South you can overwinter princess flower indoors with but a bit more difficulty than with tropical hibiscus or citrus.

Golden ray, leopard plant (*Farfugium japonicum*, formerly *Ligularia tussilaginea*)

Perennial; hardiness zones 5–9, heat-zones 9–1

Mature height: 2 to 2½ feet

Light to moderate shade, moist to wet soil

Heat-resistant perennials that will tolerate shade and poorly drained soil are rare. Golden ray and its variegated selections are little used in southern gardens but deserve more attention. The plants are very bold, with rounded or bean-shaped leaves to ten inches in diameter and tall, nearly leafless stems topped with large, golden, daisy flowers. Some of the cultivars have plain green leaves, but others are spotted or have margins penciled with a lighter color. Still others have ruffled leaf margins. In areas that suffer from extended dry spells during the summer, the ligularias should be planted along streams or pond banks, or in low areas that remain boggy all summer. If you let slugs or snails get ahead of you (they love moist soil) they can disfigure leaves of golden ray, which will remind you of your neglect each time you look their way.

Helichrysum, strawflower (*Helichrysum bracteatum*)

Most helichrysums grown as annuals; heat-zones 12–1
Mature height: 12 to 30 inches, depending on the variety
Full sun

Given excellent drainage, the annual strawflowers can withstand high heat and will bloom all summer, especially if deadheaded. When my wife and I were in the commercial herb business, we grew several rows of the variety 'Monstrosum' (a terrible name for a beautiful plant) and would send bunches of the fresh strawflowers along with shipments of fresh herbs to restaurants. The restaurants loved them for table decorations. Blossom colors range from shiny, deep purple-red through pink and yellow to white. Strawflowers are often grown for cutting when half-open, and are dried for winter bouquets. The dried stems are weak and are usually replaced with florist's wire wrapped with floral tape. The dwarf, mixed color variety 'Bright Bikinis' is quite popular, but the latest rage is the variety 'Golden Beauty', which was developed for growing in containers and hanging baskets. It has a distinctive habit of growth, with branches arching up from the base, each tipped with a golden blossom about 1½ inches in diameter. I understand that there are tender perennial helichrysums that grow in zone 9 and 10, but I haven't seen them.

Strawflower (*Helichrysum bracteatum* 'Bright Bikini Mixed Colors')

Heliotrope, cherry pie plant (*Heliotropium arborescens*)

Tender perennial; hardiness zone 11, heat-zones 12–1
Mature height: 14 to 24 inches
Full sun to light shade

Heliotrope is limited in uses because only the royal purple color is common in our country. Europeans grow pink, rose, and white varieties as well. However, where purple can be combined with just the right shade of gold, the two can make a smashing combination. The old standby variety 'Marine' now comes in a dwarf version that grows very well in containers. In midsummer, heliotrope sets on prodigious crops of flat sprays which tend to go brown in a few weeks. Get out the snips and deadhead the plants to stimulate the formation of new flowers. I am trying to interest southern nurseries in a groundcover-type, spreading, semi-hardy perennial heliotrope

Shade of purple with silver contrast: heliotrope, lavender cupflower, purple grandiflora petunias, and tall blue salvia

(*H. amplexicaule*) that I found growing wild near a long-abandoned African-American academy near North Augusta, South Carolina. It has lightly scented lavender spikes shaped like seahorses and spreads widely like the perennial verbenas. Since discovering it, I have found that it has been planted for many years in cemeteries in the Charleston, South Carolina, area. Charleston was the initial port of entry for many kinds of plant species from foreign countries, being the major east coast destination for cargo ships for much of the eighteenth century.

Hen and chicks, houseleek (*Echeveria* sp., *Sempervivum* sp.)

Semi-hardy perennials with fleshy leaves; hardiness zones 10–11, heat-zones 12–1

Mature height: 6 inches or less

Full sun, dry soil

The two different genera that include species known as "hen and chicks" are somewhat similar in growth habit. The echeverias develop many small "chicks" as offsets, which can be plugged into bare spaces when the old "hens" dry up. Their orange-red flowers, pink in some species, bloom on tall spikes, off and on throughout the summer. Cultivars have been hybridized for highly colored leaves in shades of pink, gray, and blue-green. *E. imbricata* is the most common species, often passed along among friends and family.

The sempervivums develop tight rosettes of succulent, gray-green leaves that grow dark around the pointed leaf tips late in the summer. Flower spikes of the sempervivums are tall.

Cobweb houseleeks are the bantams of hen and chicks, with rosettes seldom growing larger than a silver dollar, and many the size of marbles. Their intense blue-green, fleshy leaves are covered with "webs" of fibers. All kinds of hen and chicks demand dry soil, and will grow among rocks that heat up the soil. Accordingly, they thrive in concrete or hypertufa containers filled with potting mixes fortified with sand. In

Hen and chicks (*Sempervivum tectorum*) can withstand heat and drought, but demands good drainage. Note the bronzing that comes with age.

zones six, seven, and eight, most gardeners bring in a few small rosettes to assure a start for the following season. In the garden, the rosettes can be lost if the temperature drops below the upper twenties after an extended warm spell.

Hibiscus (*Hibiscus* sp.)

Native hibiscus species: hardy in zones 5–10, heat-zones 12–1

Tropical species must be brought indoors in zone 8 and further north; adapted to heat-zones 12–1

Mature height: to 8 feet for hardy species, to small tree size for the tropical species

Full sun to light shade

The hibiscus family may have caused more confusion among gardeners than any other. For those who associate the name only with the brilliant tropical hibiscuses they see in South Florida gardens and the very southern tip of Texas, learning that there are many more equally beautiful and perfectly hardy native *Hibiscus* species is a revelation. The native hibiscuses were restricted to the status of wildflowers until seed breeders hybridized 'Southern Belle' several years ago, and later the more compact 'Dixie Belle'. These proved to be fairly winter-hardy; I've seen them overwinter reliably in southern Michigan, where the canes freeze to ground level. New growth shoots up in early summer. 'Dixie Belle' has incredibly large blossoms for the size of the plant; to say the blossoms are the diameter of a dinner plate is no exaggeration. Its plants are bushier and thicker than those of the unimproved species, which tend to send up very tall, lanky canes. Although the native hibiscuses are marsh or streamside plants, they will grow well in average garden soil, watered only during dry spells. The tropical hibiscuses

Hibiscus **'Disco Belle' has enormous blossoms and comes in many colors.**

The native swamp denizen, wild hibiscus (*H. coccineus*), will grow well in ordinary garden soil.

don't tolerate wet feet and grow better on sandy soil or in large containers filled with moderately fast-draining potting soil. The two classes are easy to distinguish—the tropical hibiscuses have dark green, glossy leaves, and the natives have larger, gray-green, rather felty foliage. The tropicals have slightly tubular blossoms which flare open, while the native species have flat, wide-open blossoms. Both kinds, to my chagrin, have proved irresistible to deer in my garden.

Hosta (*Hosta* sp.)

Perennial; hardiness zones 3-8, heat-zones 8–1

Mature size: from 8 inches to 4 feet

Light to moderate shade

Hostas are generally regarded as unsuited to gardens in zone 8 and further south. In reality, several cultivars will perform well as far south as northern Florida, but hostas in the Deep South require more shade. Hostas grow very well in zones 6 and 7, and fairly well in 8, but the early-awakening cultivars can he hit by late frost and will look beat up until the damage is hidden by new growth. In the Midsouth and Upper South, the challenge is to keep hostas sufficiently moist during our dry summers while fighting off slugs and earwigs, both of which can disfigure hostas. The perennial plant expert John Elsley tends his shaded garden down the road a few miles from our farm and tries all the hostas offered by Wayside Gardens. The large hardwood trees in his landscape deliver some protection from late frosts and allow him to grow everything from the tiny edging cultivars to the huge, waist-high specimen hostas. Mulches and a sprinkler system help his hostas thrive.

Well-sited plant of variegated hosta at Louis and Jane Stone home garden, Donalds, SC

You will often hear it said that hostas are grown more for their foliage than for their blossoms, but just try to ignore the tall spikes of fragrant, white flowers on *H. plantaginea*, or the extremely tall lavender flower spikes on 'Krossa Regal'. They demand your attention. One of the best sources of information on hostas adapted to the South is the catalog of Plant Delights Nursery. Also, San Felasco Nursery (see Appendix) has screened the hostas for resistance to northern Florida's heat and humidity and offers only adapted cultivars.

Ice plant (hardy) (*Delosperma cooperi, D. nucifera*)
Perennial; hardiness zones 8–10, heat-zones 10–8
Mature height: 2 to 4 inches
Full sun or light shade

This little jewel qualifies as what I call a "Wow, gee whiz!" plant because it excites such comments when seen in one's garden. Although I was dubious about its hardiness when I planted it in my garden, it lasted several years, growing among piled-up boulders with a little sandy soil sifted down between them. The ground-hugging, spreading plants have tiny, fleshy leaves, and astonishingly vivid cerise blossoms with many string-thin petals extending from a contrasting disk. It should make an excellent plant for containers as it doesn't overgrow and will trail over the rims of containers. I wouldn't give it much of a chance on heavy soil where summer rainfall is high because it is native to a dry habitat. It can tolerate the salt spray that comes with a beachfront landscape. *D. nucifera* is reputedly a bit hardier than *D. cooperi*. Its flowers are smaller and yellow.

Hardy ice plant (*Delosperma cooperi*) at Norfolk Botanical Garden

Impatiens, busy Lizzie (*Impatiens walleriana, I.* × *hawkeri* hybrids)
Grown as an annual; hardiness zone 11, heat-zones 12–1
Mature height: 8 to 16 inches, depending on moisture level of the soil and the variety
Light to moderate shade

The many selections from *I. walleriana* are so neat, undemanding, and colorful that they have made impatiens the number one bedding plant in sales. They grow quite well in containers and hanging baskets, too. Sales of New Guinea hybrids, based on the genes of *I. hawkeri* and other species, help to swell the total. At one time, the New Guinea hybrids were touted as sun tolerant, but they don't do nearly as well in full sun in the South as they do in the North. Recently, yellow and orange-flowered species were thrown into the impatiens gene pool to produce the 'Seashells' color series. Its cultivars have descending branches and nodding, cupped blossoms in yellow, coral, apricot, and papaya colors. Actually, the hardest problem when buying impatiens for gardens or containers is boiling down the

**Variegated New Guinea impatiens, Holloway garden,
Greenwood, SC**

list to the varieties that look good together.
The job is easier with standard impatiens
because all their colors are soft. It's only in
the New Guinea hybrids that you
encounter the socko scarlet, orange, and
deep purple colors and strongly variegated
foliage that complicate matchmaking. Whichever
impatiens you buy, grow them on the lean side,
and water them lightly but frequently, not to the point
of starvation or wilting, but with just enough plant food and water to
keep them from growing tall and leggy.

Indian blanket, blanket flower (*Gaillardia pulchella, G. grandiflora*)

Indian blanket (*G. pulchella*) is annual, adapted to heat-zones 12–1

G. *grandiflora* is perennial; hardiness zones 3-8, heat-zones 8–1

Mature height of the annuals: 1 to 2 feet; perennials: 8 inches to 2 feet

Full sun, dry soil

If there is a tougher, more adaptable flower than
these native species, I have yet to see it. We scattered gaillardia seeds on the barren subsoil
remaining after we tore down a greenhouse.
Weeds wouldn't grow, but the gaillardia
flourished! You may have seen Indian blanket covering roadsides in Texas and
Oklahoma after the bluebonnets and
prairie coreopsis have peaked. It's quite a
sight—acres and acres of the yellow, gold, and
mahogany bicolored, daisy blossoms, blooming
right through summer, given the occasional rain
shower. Gaillardia will grow on sandy or clay soil, and per-
sists from volunteer seedlings. *Wildflowers of Texas* says that
Indian blanket will also grow in "sand or shell along the
coast." Southern seacoast flowers are few and far between.

**Blanket flower
(*Gaillardia pulchella*)
is a tough and durable
reseeding annual.**

You can get seeds of straight yellow or red colors of gaillardia, or varieties with double flowers, but I think that much of its charm is in the
infinite variety of color combinations of the single-flowered, unimproved species. Grow gaillardia from plants or from direct-seeding in
the garden. The perennial species blooms quite early.

Ironweed (*Vernonia altissima*)

Perennial; native to much of the eastern USA; hardiness zones 5–9, heat-zones 9–1, best adapted to zones 6 through 8

Mature height: 4 to 8 feet (on moist, fertile soil)

Full sun to light shade

In the wild, you are most likely to find ironweed growing along streams and in boggy spots. Near our farm, in a low area where spring water seeps even during extended droughts, ironweed grows quite tall and puts on a great show of distinctive, reddish-purple blossoms in flat clusters. It comes and goes just before the wild asters of late fall color up. This long, lean country cousin can fit into city landscapes as well as country bogs. It adapts nicely to moist garden soils. Set ironweed plants in the back of woodland edges where you won't have to walk around the plants. There is no way to hasten blooming; you just have to wait until the nights are about the same length as days before ironweed does its thing. The blossoms are visited by many butterfly species.

Jasmine (*Jasminum* sp., *Trachelospermum* sp.)

J. humile is the hardiest, zones 7–9, heat-zones 9–7. *J. officinale*: hardiness zones 9–10, heat-zones 10–8; *T. jasminoides*: hardiness zones 9–10, heat-zones 10–6

Mature height: to 20 feet for vines, 4 feet for shrubs

Full sun to light shade

Fragrant climbing jasmine (*Jasminium polyanthum*)

PLANT PICS

As a class, the many jasmines are highly popular landscape plants. However, most of them are so tender that they won't survive winters north of hardiness zone 9, and many of them flower during the winter and early spring. Among the best summer-flowering jasmines are the common white jasmine (*J. officinale*), Italian jasmine (*J. humile*), and confederate jasmine (*T. jasminoides*). Common white jasmine is a tall, twining vine with fragrant, white, pinwheel-shaped blossoms about one inch in diameter in spring and early summer. With protection, it can survive winters in zone 7b. Italian jasmine is a large, evergreen shrub with small, fragrant, yellow blossoms all summer long. It has long, whippy branches that can be nipped off to keep the plant in bounds. Confederate jasmine is a clambering vine that can be used as a groundcover. It has small, white, fragrant flowers that resemble those of true jasmine and peak in spring and early summer. It is hardy in zone 9 and further south. Even though certain of the jasmines are used as groundcovers, I can't recommend them. It is difficult to navigate through the vines without tripping, and dried leaves tend to blow in among them and collect as unsightly litter. You ever try to rake leaves out of vining groundcovers? Most gardeners capitulate, set their mower high, butch-cut the vines, then rake up the mess. Traumatic, but it works.

Jessamine, Carolina jessamine (*Gelsemium sempervirens*)

Flowering, woody, perennial vine; hardiness zones 7–9, heat-zones 9–7

Mature height: to 20 feet, higher when growing in forests

Full sun to moderate shade

The beauty of this early-blooming, near-evergreen vine belies the fact that all parts of it are poisonous if ingested. It has shiny, dark green leaves about two inches long and slender tendrils that wave in the wind. Masses of small, yellow, very fragrant, tubular blooms begin to show at daffodil time, or earlier during mild winters. We have a particularly ugly utility pole in the back yard and planted jessamine to hide it. It hit the top of the pole some time ago and now is tightrope-walking along the wires. One of these days the whole caboodle may short out and blow up with a flash and a loud bang, but I don't want to cut the vines. We would probably add the double-flowered cultivar 'Augusta' and the winter-flowering cultivars of *G. rankinii* to our landscape if we had more utility poles. By the way, jessamine is not related to the many jasmines (*Jasminum* sp.) and is the state flower of South Carolina.

Carolina jessamine (*Gelsemium sempervirens***)**
PLANT PICS

Joe-Pye weed (*Eupatorium purpureum*)

Perennial, native to much of the East; hardiness zones 3-9, heat-zones
9–1

Height: 5 feet for the dwarf cultivars to 8 feet or more for the species

Full sun or light shade

Joe-Pye weed
(*Eupatorium
purpureum*) now
comes in pink,
purple, white,
and rose colors.

In the wild, you are likely to find Joe-Pye growing in the same low, wet areas as ironweed, and often in high shade along the edges of open, moist woodlands. The dusty lavender-pink of its huge, flat clusters of blossoms is easier to work with than the vivid purple of ironweed, so more breeding work has been done on Joe-Pye. Consequently, you can buy cultivars that mature at shoulder height, and bloom a week or so earlier than the species. Still, you won't see color until late summer. Joe-Pye will grow quite well in regular garden soil, particularly if you spread mulch around the plants. It is an irresistible nectar source for many species of butterflies and hummingbirds. You may wish to stake your plants; the weight of the blossoms can bend them over, particularly after rainstorms. It's a good thing that butterflies don't weigh much or their sheer numbers would bend the plants double!

Joseph's coat (*Amaranthus tricolor, Alternanthera ficoidea*)

Amaranthus tricolor is annual; *Alternanthera ficoidea* is a tender
perennial, grown as an annual; hardy through zone 9, heat-zones
12–1

Mature height: 4 to 6 feet for amaranthus, 1 foot for alternanthera

Full sun for amaranthus; alternanthera prefers full sun but will
tolerate light shade

Luckily for us gardeners, only two species share the attractive common name of Joseph's coat. However, they could hardly be more different. *Amaranthus tricolor* is a tall, slim plant with large, rough leaves in theatrical shades of green, bronze, cerise, orange, scarlet, and cream. In some varieties the terminal foliage is an intense, almost fluorescent pink. It grows better from direct-seeding than from transplants, unless the seedlings are quite small when set out. The plants tend to dominate landscapes and are best planted in beds by themselves as visual focal points. *A. ficoidea* is most often massed in close

Joseph's Coat (*Amaranthus tricolor* 'Molten Fire'), Park Seed Co. trials

plantings and sheared low to form patterns in floral clocks and other designs. Several dwarf cultivars with small leaves are available. Few other heat-resistant foliage plants have the vivid variegations of alternanthera, in red, green, cream, and pink shades. Also, few others can tolerate the severe pruning required to keep the plants very low. Alternanthera is often used in topiary animals for color accents among the ivy and creeping fig plants that simulate pelts, and as a trailer in containers.

Lamb's ears (*Stachys byzantina*)

Perennial; hardiness zones 4–8, heat-zones 8–1
Mature height: to 14 inches
Full sun

I've grown the sprawling, common lamb's ears for many years for the felty, silvery leaves that give it its common name. But after growing 'Big Ears' (originally known as 'Countess Helene von Stein') for a few seasons, I much prefer the latter. It has larger leaves, mounded plants, and a denser habit of growth than traditional lamb's ears. True, the foliage is not quite as silvery nor as felty, but the plants are much neater, albeit larger in diameter, up to two feet for me. Use 'Big Ears' for edging or for silvery contrast among perennials or shrubs. Flower spikes will shoot up late in the season but the blossoms are plain. Cut and dry the spikes for winter arrangements before they stress the plant. Give stachys good drainage and protection from slugs and snails.

Giant lamb's ear or big ears (*Stachys byzantina* 'Countess Helene von Stein'), Park Seed Co. trials

Lantana (*Lantana camara*, *L. montevidensis*, and hybrids)

Semi-hardy perennial, blooms from spring through fall; official hardiness zone 11, heat-zone adaptability zones 12–1
Mature height: to 6 feet for the bush type, to 12 inches for the trailing hybrids
Full sun

Along the Gulf Coast, lantana doesn't get much respect. The blue-black berries that make it attractive during fall and winter are

**Yellow lantana
(*L. camara*)
Linden
Plantation,
Vicksburg,
Mississippi**

vectored by birds throughout landscapes and open land. All parts of lantana are poisonous to humans if ingested, and the foliage can irritate the skin of some people. Yet, despite its negatives, lantana is extremely resistant to heat, humidity, and drought, and is one of the best butterfly flowers. *L. camara* is native to Florida and South Georgia. It has bushy plants with flat clusters of yellow or orange blossoms, sometimes flushed with pink. The bushy cultivar 'Miss Huff', selected from *L. camara*, is hardy in zone 7b and can overwinter in zone 6 if cut back and mulched with at least six inches of pinestraw. The hybrids from *L. montevidensis* are less hardy but more appealing to many gardeners because the flowers are purple, blue, and white, and the trailing plants are tailor-made for hanging baskets. Now, hybridization has broadened the range of flower colors in both the trailing and bush types. Two of the newest patented cultivars are the FloraStar winner 'Patriot Hot Country' (reddish-orange) and 'Patriot Hallelujah' (yellow-gold). A new series named 'Cowboy' has compact plants. When choosing which plants of lantana to take home, reject the robust types with few flowers in comparison to foliage. Go for the compact plants that are loaded with flowers; they will give you a better show over the summer.

Lily turf, mondo grass (*Liriope* sp., *Ophiopogon* sp.)

Semi-hardy perennials, hardiness zones 6–10, heat-zones 10–1
Mature height: 6 to 24 inches, depending on the species
Full sun or light shade for lily turf, moderate shade for mondo grass

I've combined the descriptions for two different plants here because they are used for the same purposes and home gardeners often aren't sure which is which. Plant breeders have selected many cultivars of the grasslike lily turf (*Liriope muscari*). Most have dark green leaves and lavender flowers. Some have been selected for a compact habit and will not grow tall or spread widely. Others were selected for variegated leaves. I have the yellow and green variegated cultivar 'Silvery Sunproof'. It freezes to the ground during winter, but survives. The evergreen mondo grass cultivars look somewhat like lily turf in foliage and flowers, except for the handsome little

Lily turf (*Liriope muscari*) PLANT PICS

dwarf mondo grass, which is quite distinct, with narrow, dark green leaves in dense clumps. Black mondo grass (*O. planiscapus* 'Nigrescens') is the least hardy of the group, but should survive in zone 8 and further south, and perhaps through 7b. It is a beautiful plant, with dark, purple-green leaves and pinkish-white sprays of flowers. You can use either lily turf or mondo grass in edgings or containers, but check with your nurseryman if you want a groundcover. Only certain cultivars will knit together to cover the ground solidly.

Lotus (*Nelumbo lutea, N. nucifera*)

N. lutea is a native perennial; hardiness zones 4–11, heat-zones 12–1.

N. nucifera is less hardy; I've seen it overwinter in deep ponds in Natchez, Mississippi.

Mature height above the surface of water: 2 to 3 feet

Full sun or light shade

Lotus is a great plant for large water gardens (wait, let's make that *very* large water gardens). The crowns spread like crazy, and it is a big, messy job to remove them. Yet, they have such an opulent appearance that many gardeners just turn them loose in a pool and let them commandeer it. The yellow-flowered American lotus (*N. lutea*) is the hardier of the two, but Indian lotus (*N. nucifera*) offers more variety in blossom colors and forms, with pink, white, and deep rose colors, and double-flowered cultivars. Lotus leaves are large, gray-green, wavy-edged, and are held above the surface of the water. The long-stemmed, very large, fragrant flowers are followed by salt-shaker seed pods that flower arrangers covet. Where pond water freezes you should plant lotus roots well below the expected ice level; they can't stand freezing.

Lotus, Indian or Chinese (*Nelumbo nucifera*), Natchez, Mississippi

Louisiana iris (Complex hybrids developed from species native to the Gulf Coast and lower Mississippi Valley)

Perennial across the South, but mulching is advised in zones 6 and 7; hardiness zones 6–9, heat-zones 9–3

Mature height: 3 to 6 feet

Full sun in zones 6 and 7, light shade further south

Any southerner who loves bearded irises but resents the care they require should try the native Louisiana iris. Barbara Perry Lawton in her landmark book, *Magic of Irises*, describes them thusly: "Marvelous plants for a bog or water garden, the Louisiana irises are also handsome choices for herbaceous beds or borders. They are beautiful as cut flowers and easy to arrange." Nearly the full range of iris colors is represented among the Louisiana hybrids, but their large blossoms are flatter and more open than those of the bearded class. While it is true that they will grow in boggy soil or on hummocks in standing water, Louisiana irises will adapt willingly to garden soil kept moist and mulched. They can tolerate hot, humid weather and suffer from fewer insect and disease problems than bearded irises. When cut for display in vases, buds will continue to open for several days. Louisiana irises are heavy feeders and should be fertilized three times yearly, in spring, summer, and fall. Early summer is peak bloom time. Another iris well worth growing in the Upper South is the diminutive, early-blooming crested iris (*I. cristata*). It grows best in woodland situations, where it spreads into drifts.

Louisiana iris growing on a pond bank at Baton Rouge

Mandevilla (*Mandevilla splendens*)

Frost-tender perennial vine, heat-zones 12–1

Mature height: to 20 feet in the Deep South

Full sun or light shade

It is a rare southern gardener who does not know mandevilla. It began showing up as a trellised container plant in the Middle and Upper South during the 1980s and has become very popular. Gardeners are most familiar with the deep-pink-flowered, high climbing variety 'Alice du Pont'. It can grow ten feet or more in a single season and will be covered with blossoms all summer long.

Mandevilla is hardy in zone 8 and further south; further north you can cut it back and store the plants indoors during the winter. You should try the new bush cultivars that are commonly called "dipladenia." They include the patented 'Scarlet Pimpernel' and 'Faire Lady', and the longer-established favorites, 'Red Riding Hood' and the white-flowered 'Summer Snow'. The bush types tend to throw out short tendrils which you can either nip off or allow to ramble, depending on whether you want a bush or a trailing plant for hanging basket use.

Closeup of the large blossoms of mandevilla

Marigold, Triploid (*Tagetes patula*, *T. erecta*)

Annual, sets no seeds, thus will not volunteer; heat-zones 12–1

Mature height: 12 to 16 inches

Full sun or light shade

Unlike the short, genetic diploid French marigolds and some of the taller, erect African marigolds, the triploids continue to bloom through hot weather and don't blank. ("Blank" is the term seedsmen use to describe marigolds that continue growing but don't bloom during very hot weather.) The continuous blooming of triploids is partly due to their vigor but more because the plants are sterile and don't set seeds. Seed breeders such as Floranova have overcome one of the big problems with the triploids, dating back to when the W. Atlee Burpee Company led the field in developing them. The problem then was in seed germination; it was slow and weak. Now the problem has been solved, and triploid plants are priced at just a slight premium over other hybrid marigolds. Named varieties are available in the typical yellow, gold, orange, and mahogany bicolors. A recent introduction, 'Zenith Red', brings a brick red color to the triploids. All the triploid marigolds have double flowers, which means they have several layers of petals. While best suited to bedding, the triploid marigolds also grow well in large containers. Keep an eye out for spider mites and spray hot spots before they spread. The 1999

"French" marigold (*Tagetes patula* 'Bonanza Bolero')

All-America Selections award winner 'Bonanza Bolero' is not a triploid but, surprisingly, performs about as well in the South. It is a vigorous French type that doesn't grow leggy. All the French marigolds are well suited to container culture. By the way, one of the most enduring myths of urban folklore is that marigolds repel insects. They don't, but just try to convince true believers!

Melampodium, butter daisy (*Leucanthemum paludosum*, formerly *Melampodium paludosum*)

Perennial, but usually grown as an annual; hardiness zones 6–9, heat-zones 9–3

Mature height: 1½ to 3 feet, depending on the variety

Full sun

Butter daisy (*Melampodium paludosum*), Park Seed Co. trials

This is a relative newcomer among seed-grown, heat-resistant annuals. Gardeners began to see it at botanical gardens about twenty years ago, and garden centers began to keep plants in inventory. Were it not for the extraordinary resistance of melampodium to heat, humidity, and summer thunderstorms, it might still be an obscure curiosity. It offers only one color, yellow, on unremarkable plants. But does it bloom! All summer long, with no time-outs to catch its breath. The first varieties brought in were rather leggy and a bit sparse in flowers, but the compact 'Showstar' has a much improved ratio of flowers to foliage.

Mexican bush salvia, Mexican Bush Sage (*Salvia leucantha*)

Perennial in all southern zones, but needs a pinestraw mulch in zone 6; official hardiness zone rating is 10–11, heat-zone 12–1

Mature height: to 6 feet on large, old plants on fertile soil. Four feet is the average.

Full sun

I listed this salvia separately from the others because of its importance. Everyone, it seems, loves this large, late-summer-blooming subshrub. In zone 7 the top freezes to the ground but the roots survive all but the most severe winters. Further south, the plants will freeze back partially. Each year the "plot thickens" as the crown of the mother plant increases in size and adds more canes. An estab-

Mexican bush salvia (*Salvia leucantha*) in Wilson garden

lished plant can grow to six or eight feet across and can bear dozens of long, furry blossom spikes that hold their color until hard frost. I've seen three variations in colors: reddish purple with white markings, violet-blue with white markings, and recently I saw a brownish red with white highlights. *The Southern Living Garden Book* states there is a pink-flowered variety. To my knowledge there are no named cultivars, and many bushes are grown from passalong plants. Near my house, in an abandoned herb field, a bush has grown among the tall fescue grass for ten years with no irrigation, water, or fertilizer. It's a tough customer, yet in fresh or dried flower arrangements you couldn't ask for a more elegant flower. Butterflies flock to it.

Mexican heather, cigar plant (*Cuphea hyssopifolia, C. ignea*)

> Semi-hardy subshrubs. *C. ignea*: hardiness zones 10–11, heat-zones 12–1; *C. hyssopifolia*: less hardy, but has the same heat-zone rating
>
> Mature height: 1 to 2 feet
>
> Full sun or light shade

During recent years, Mexican heather (*C. hyssopifolia*) has become quite popular for edgings and as a small, self-contained shrub for containers. It has very small, glossy, dark green leaves and many tiny flowers in light blue, purple, pink, or white. In zone eight and further north the top growth will freeze, but plants will sometimes come back from the roots. Cigar plant (*C. ignea*) seldom exceeds eighteen inches in height and has dull green leaves and slim, bright red blossoms tipped with creamy white. A gray rim around the very tip completes the cigar image. Both species are quite resistant to heat and humidity, but Mexican heather is far and away the more popular of the two.

Bacopa '**Snowstorm' in foreground, with purple-flowered Mexican heather (*Cuphea hyssopifolia*)**

Mexican or Spanish tarragon (*Tagetes lucida*)

Semi-hardy perennial, overwinters in zone 7 and south; heat-zones 12–1

Mature height: 2 to 2½ feet

Full sun

Anise-scented marigold or Mexican tarragon (*Tagetes lucida*) has an intense anise fragrance and flavor.

When we gave tours of our herb farm and encouraged visitors to smell and taste the various herbs, Mexican tarragon was everyone's favorite. They loved the intense anise scent of the foliage. It was hard for them to believe that it was truly a marigold because tours ended in late summer, and the plants don't bloom until the cusp of fall. Lengthening nights shift the plant into its flowering cycle, bringing many-flowered clusters of small, single, yellow blossoms. They are unmistakably marigolds, with ray petals, tufted disks and all. The plants are clump-forming, erect, and have long, semi-evergreen, willowlike leaves that turn from dark green to bronze with the coming of fall. While technically an herb, Mexican tarragon doesn't have to play second fiddle to garden flowers but can hold its own for beauty. And as a bonus, you can eat the flowers; they taste like they smell, only with a slight bitter overtone.

Million Bells™, calibrachoa (*Calibrachoa* sp.)

Semi-hardy perennial, usually grown as an annual; hardiness zones 10–11, heat-zones 12–1

Trails to 3 feet

Full sun or, in the Deep South, light shade

I had this relative newcomer pegged as a near-petunia until I took a close look at it. True, it may have long ago sprung from the same family tree as petunias, but the resemblance is superficial. Its blossoms are much smaller than multiflora petunias and are more entire, meaning that they are not deeply lobed or divid-

A lovely example of *Calibrachoa* 'Million Bells' at Weidner's Greenhouses. Note the trailing habit.

ed. The blossoms have a tidy habit of dropping off when they have faded. Its leaves are much smaller than those of petunias. The color range is limited at present—red, blue, pink, and white—but will be expanded shortly. Million Bells makes a near-perfect plant for containers and hanging baskets, staying low while trailing down about two feet, and dripping with blossoms. A competing brand with somewhat larger flowers is sold as Lyricashowers.

Montbretia, crocosmia (*Crocosmia masoniorum* and hybrids with *C. crocosmiiflora*)

> Bulbous perennials. *C. masoniorum*: hardiness zones 7–9, heat-zones 9–7; *C. crocosmiiflora*: hardiness zones 6–9, heat-zones 9–6.
>
> Mature height: 2 to 4 feet
>
> Full sun

The montbretias, called "tritonias" at one time, are old-fashioned flowers that keep coming back for years. They have slender, gladiola-like foliage. After a few years, if undisturbed, individual bulbs will naturalize and thicken into drifts. At one time the colors were harsh, and some still come in shocking shades of scarlet and orange, but a clear yellow hybrid is available as well. Technically, the species that more closely resembles gladioli is commonly called montbretia, while the name crocosmia is used for the species with a flower spike that bends at an angle like bird of paradise flower. None of the species or hybrids bloom all summer, but their peak color comes in midsummer when colorful flowers are especially appreciated. The plants stay in bloom for three to five weeks, and the long-stemmed sprays can be cut for vases. A scarlet crocosmia resembling the variety 'Lucifer' has escaped all along the roadsides in New Zealand. Blue lily of the Nile fled gardens at the same time and hangs out with it—one of the prettiest accidental combinations you'll see anywhere.

Crocosmia or montbretia (*Crocosmia masoniorum*) with blue lily of the Nile (*Agapanthus orientalis*) at Rathmoy estate, Hunterville, New Zealand

Pampas grass (*Cortaderia selloana*)

Hardy except at high elevations; official hardiness zones 7–10, heat-
zones 10–7

Mature height: 6 feet in the Upper South to 10 feet or more in the
Deep South, 3 to 4 feet for the dwarf cultivars, 6 to 8 feet for
standard varieties

Full sun

I dithered for some time about listing a number of ornamental grasses among my favorites, but to be honest, I don't care for any of them except pampas grass and some of the native species like the wispy muhly grass, *Muhlenbergia capillaris.* Clumps of pampas grass have become horticultural clichés, I realize, but no other grass can match them for making a statement gracefully and memorably. Its plants come in either male or female sexes, and the female plumes are much showier than those of the male. Unfortunately, like waiting for a holly to set fruit before knowing for sure that it is a female, you have to see the flowers on pampas grass to tell its gender, unless your supplier pre-sorts them. Plumes may be silvery white, creamy white, or even flushed with pink. If you see red and black plumes on the same plant you will know you are in South Carolina, where diehard Gamecock fans have been known to resort to spray cans to advertise their team's colors. It doesn't hurt pampas grass to cut it to near the ground in late winter, but the tough stems will wipe the edge off a chainsaw in no time flat. To simplify cutting back clumps, ingenious gardeners throw a rope with a slip knot around the clump and pull it tight. It holds the topgrowth together so you can get to the canes more easily. For a dwarf pampas grass that is hardy through zone 6b, try *C. selloana* 'Pumila'.

Pepper (ornamental) (*Capsicum annuum*)

Tropical perennial, usually grown as an annual; heat-zones 12–1

Mature height of ornamental varieties 1 to 2 feet

Full sun

When I saw ornamental peppers begin to come on the market about thirty years ago, I thought they would take the South like Grant took Richmond. Didn't happen. Turned out that the major botanical gardens liked their looks but were afraid of public liability suits from parents whose children picked and ate the hot fruits. You

can't blame the kids; the fruits are most attractive—they come in shades of red, yellow, purple, and green, some with contrasting markings. They can be round, tapered, cigar-
shaped, curved like cows' horns, twisted,
or tucked into themselves. Most varieties
are pungent (that's the term that pepper-
ologists prefer over "hot") and kids have a
way of sampling them when they are a city
block away from a water fountain. All the negatives aside, the little plants are colorful from late
spring through fall. They are very resistant to heat and
humidity and are troubled less by pepper diseases and
insects than sweet peppers. One of my favorites is
'Midnight Express', with purple and white foliage and glossy, deep
purple fruits.

Ornamental pepper 'Alladin'

Perennial pinks, cheddar pinks, dianthus

(*Dianthus gratianopolitanus*)

> Perennial zones 4–9, but short-lived zone 8 and further
> south; heat-zones 9–1
> Mature height of flower stems: 6 to 8 inches
> Full sun or light shade

In general, the perennial pinks are not
well suited to the South, as they tend to
melt away under high heat and frequent
summer rains. Some, however, provide
attractive silver-blue foliage year-round
and a brief but spectacular show of bloom
in the spring and fall. Foremost among these
is the cheddar pink group, and especially the
one-foot high 'Bath's Pink'. Other cultivars within
this species range in height from four to eight inches
and offer red, pink, or white blossoms. San Felasco
Nurseries (see page 127) likes the cultivar 'Firewitch'
for season-long color. Cheddar pinks are adapted to growing in
containers and in sandy soil, or in raised beds for improved
drainage. Certain of the cheddar pink cultivars breathe the clove
fragrance so familiar from carnations.

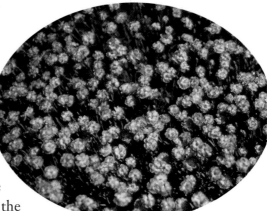

Cheddar pink (*Dianthus gratianopolitanus*)

Periwinkle, Madagascar periwinkle (*Catharanthus roseus*)

Annual, zone 10 and further north, short-lived perennial further south; heat-zones 12–1

Mature height: 10 to 14 inches

Full sun or light shade

Periwinkle
(*Catharanthus roseus* 'Pacifica Blush White')

Often confusingly called "Vinca" on labels and in catalogs, periwinkle is a southern staple. While it isn't the most heat-resistant flower for ground beds and containers, it comes close to it. For years, the most popular varieties of periwinkle had globe shaped or slightly spreading plants. Now, from Waller Flowerseed breeders comes a large-flowered *trailing* periwinkle named 'Mediterranean'. It doesn't begin to trail until late summer, but between then and fall frost its branches can reach almost two feet in length. Several colors in the 'Mediterranean' series will be forthcoming. Watch for them in hanging baskets. Not to be outdone, other flower breeders are releasing new colors and larger flowers on compact plants of periwinkle. Some outstanding color series are 'Pacifica', 'Heatwave', 'Tropicana', 'Blue Pearl', and the somewhat taller 'Little' series. Periwinkle will tolerate moderately acid soil but not wet feet. Grow it in full sun with good drainage. Mulch containers with pebbles to reduce soil splash and the possibility of foliage diseases.

Persian shield (*Strobilanthes dyeranus*)

Tender perennial, grown as an annual; heat-zones 12–8

Mature height: 3 to 4 feet, taller in the Deep South

Light to mottled shade

Houseplants are jumping the fence and showing up in outdoor containers. Persian shield is an excellent example. It has long, furrowed leaves with sawtooth edges. Purple is their base color, but it is overlaid with a sheen of silver and pink, sometimes green. The plants are open and rather ungainly, which suggests planting a vine with them, perhaps blue clock vine. Or, you can plant Persian shield in a large hanging basket and let it flop over the rim.

At Fearrington Village, a resort in North Carolina, I saw a beautiful, erect specimen in a corner where it was protected from wind. It

Persian shield (*Strobilanthus dyeranus*)

appeared to have had the branch tips pinched out to encourage branching. Maybe that's the secret to keeping the plants symmetrical. If you like the theatrical in plants, try Persian shield. It is quite easy to grow, and being a tropical foliage plant, will stay in color all summer. The tubular violet-blue flowers are pretty but are outshone by the iridescent foliage.

Petunia ('Wave' color series) (*Petunia* sp.)

Annual, zone 8 and further north; short-lived perennial further south;
  heat-zones 12–1
Mature height: 4 to 6 inches; spread: 3 to 4 feet.
Full sun or light shade

'Purple Wave' won an All-America Selections award and washed across the American landscape a few years back. It caught everyone's attention with its vigorous, prostrate, spreading growth and bold color. Its originator, PanAmerican Seed Company, then followed with 'Pink Wave', 'Misty Lilac Wave', 'Coral Wave', and 'Rose Wave'. The 'Wave' petunias can be used as annual groundcovers or planted in large containers to trail over the edge. 'Wave' petunias grow so rapidly that they need frequent feeding and watering to maintain top appearance. Seeds are available to home gardeners, and 'Wave' petunias are also distributed as plugs, which are small, pre-started plants that are grown to market size by local growers. In the Deep South, petunias frequently live through the winter, but you are better off pulling out the survivors and starting afresh with vigorous, clean, new plants. In my opinion no other class of petunias delivers the combination of low, spreading plant habit, all-season bloom, and vigor of the 'Waves'. At present, they vary a little in plant height among varieties, but I expect that seed breeders will iron out the wrinkles shortly.

'Purple wave' and 'Misty Lilac Wave' were interplanted in this bed of petunias.

Petunias (other seed-grown or vegetatively-propagated types) (Petunia Hybrids)

Semi-hardy perennials, mostly grown as annuals; hardy through zone
    9, may live in mild winters in zone 8; heat-zones 12–1
Mature height: 6 to 12 inches
Full sun

With my advocacy of 'Wave' petunias, I hope I haven't created the impression that gardens can get by without other types. Landscapes need the many plant habits and blossom colors and forms supplied by the plethora of hybrid petunias in the multiflora, grandiflora, and Milliflora types. In general, the multifloras, which have slightly smaller blossoms than the grandifloras, are better suited to southern climates. They have greater resistance to foliage diseases such as botrytis mold, and the sheer number of blossoms they support make you forget their relatively small size. Yet, when you go shopping, you will probably gravitate to the grandifloras on display as bedding plants because, even when quite small, the plants develop large blossoms. On the contrary, the 'Fantasy' color series within the Milliflora class are miniature in both plant and blossom size, but while as cute as a bug's ear, can't stand up long to extremes of heat, rain, and drought. They and many other outstanding petunia hybrids were developed by Goldsmith Seeds. You will probably see Supertunias as well; they are vegetatively propagated for uniformity and freedom from latent plant viruses. Swelling the crowd are the trailing Surfinia color series which include genes from the wild species for additional tolerance to weather extremes.

Creeping petunia (P. integrifolia) has somewhat larger flowers and plants than Million Bells.

I have only a few suggestions to guide you when shopping for petunia plants. Consider the plant habit—some hybrids are balcony or cascade types, which have robust plants that trail. They display best in hanging baskets, large pots, and planter boxes. And when combining petunia colors in beds, stick to either multifloras or grandifloras; don't mix the two types. You may be tempted to buy a number of colors and make a patchwork bed. If you do, wrap a unifying edging of a single color of petunias or another flower species around them. During recent years, *Petunia integrifolia*, a small-flowered lavender or white, semi-hardy perennial species, has become popular for hanging baskets in the Lower South. It is hardy in zones 9 through 11 and adapted to 12 through 1.

Pincushion flower (*Scabiosa caucasica*)

Perennial throughout the South; hardiness zones 4–9, heat-zones 9–1
Mature height: to 2 feet, slightly higher in Upper South
Afternoon shade in zones 8 and further south, full sun elsewhere

Horticulturists are just now beginning to test the many hardy perennials for tolerance to heat and humidity in the South. One of their happy discoveries was the performance of the perennial scabiosa in stressful weather. In zone 7 and further north they bloom intermittently all summer long. Further south they bloom from fall through winter and until very hot weather comes in early summer. The large, intricate, fully double blossoms are carried on long, nearly leafless stems, which can be tucked into vases of cut flowers. The perennial types come in blue or white. If you want the full range of flower colors—purple, red, blue, pink, and white—plant the annual *S. atropurpurea* for spring bloom in zones 6 and 7, or for fall or spring bloom further south.

Pincushion flower (*Scabiosa columbaria* 'Butterfly Blue')

Plectranthus, Swedish ivy, iboza (*Plectranthus* sp.)

Frost-tender perennial; heat-zones 12–6
Mature height: to 3 feet, but the trailing types are
    more common
Light to moderate shade

Of the several species of *Plectranthus*, three are often for sale in southern garden centers and are recommended as foliage plants for growing in pots and hanging baskets. Their tolerance for shade makes them especially desirable. Most often seen is the green and white, trailing, variegated form of *P. forsteri*, sometimes labeled *P. iboza*. Next in popularity is Brazilian coleus (White Flower Farms identifies it as *P. argentatus*), which has considerably larger leaves than the variegated type. Its foliage is a

Plectranthus sp., **green-and-white variegated**

Plectranthus sp., dark purple

Brazilian coleus (*Plectranthus* sp.), Holloway home garden, Greenwood, SC

silvery blue-gray and is slightly puckered. Its plants are erect rather than low and spreading like *P. coleoides*. It is native to Australia, halfway around the world from Brazil. Third in popularity is the smaller, green-leafed, heavily-flowered type that was so popular during the days of flower children and macramé plant hangers. It was known as Swedish ivy. I think it is *P. oertendahlii*, but navigating the shoals of *Plectranthus* is like entering a roomful of strangers without name tags. Occasionally offered is a camphor-scented plectranthus commonly called Vick's plant, in reference to its medicinal odor, but being plain green and with small, thick, somewhat wavy leaves, it doesn't have much visual appeal.

Plumbago (*Plumbago auriculata*)

Perennial zones 9–10, heat-zones 10–1

Mature height: 3 to 4 feet in zones 6 and 7, to 20 feet in zones 8 and further south

Full sun

So many powder-blue blossoms cover the plants of plumbago from midsummer on that you can hardly see the foliage. You can buy cultivars with white or deep blue flowers if you like, but I prefer the lighter

Plumbago (*P. auriculata*) at Cottonwood Estate, Panmurie, New Zealand

blue. The blossoms come in clusters that will remind you of blue phlox, *P. divaricata*. In my zone 7 garden, we start with new plants each year except when, after a very mild winter, volunteer seedlings sprout around the mother plant. Our plants tend to flop, so we tie them to supports. Further south, they can climb quite high, but they take two or three years to reach full height. The vines don't twine, and need tying up. I've seen them used as groundcovers, but I can't imagine trying to get through the tangle of vines to pull the errant weed. Plumbago needs good drainage and responds well to mulches if they are kept away from the crown of the plants. The so-called "dwarf plumbago" (*Ceratostigma plumbaginoides*) is not a true plumbago, but is a shade plant of uncommon beauty.

Polka dot plant (*Hypoestes phyllostachya*)

> Tender perennial, usually grown as an annual; hardiness zone 11, heat-zones 12–6
>
> Mature height: to 3 feet in the Deep South, much shorter further north
>
> Light to moderate shade

Plant breeding projects can become quite costly, thus hybridizers tend to concentrate on species with proven potential. However, a plant breeder took a chance on a then little-known shade plant a few years back, and produced a winner. Polka dot plant has insignificant purple flowers, but gardeners don't mind. The foliage is so attractive that it can carry the day. The 'Splash' color series of *Hypoestes* comes in pink, white, or deep rose leaves, all with contrasting dark green veins. Their foliage can brighten dark corners in the garden. The plants keep on growing during warm weather, and in zone nine and further south, will set roots wherever branches touch the ground. Seedlings also volunteer from dropped seeds. Polka dot plant grows well in containers and looks good in combination with flowering plants. It is one of the flowers I look for when demonstrating planting containers for growing in the shade. Irrigate plantings of polka dot plant lightly every few days during prolonged dry weather.

The pink highlights of polka dot plant (*Hypoestes phyllostachya* 'Pink Splash') shine in shaded locations.

Portulaca, rose moss (*Portulaca grandiflora*)

Annual, all zones, prolific reseeder; heat-zones 12–1
Mature height: 8 to 10 inches
Full sun

"I'm in love again!" I heard a lady exclaim. She was visiting the Park Seed flower performance trials and had come upon a row of 'Sundial Peach' portulaca, a 1999 All-America Selections award winner. It was early morning and the sun was backlighting the thin petals and bringing out the delectable color. Portulaca colors have always been clear and vibrant, but never before in such a range of hues and tints, nor present in fully-double flowers. The advanced technology used to produce hybrids nowadays has made fully-double plants possible, with few single-flowered plants to detract from the effect. To top it off, the blossoms of 'Sundial' stay open longer and won't close up, except on very dark days. Its only problem is that when it re-seeds, which is often and abundantly, the seedlings won't come true, but will revert to the parents of the hybrid, and intergrades. Portulaca prefers dry, sandy, or gravelly soil, and will tolerate prolonged high heat. When grown on heavy soil, it will do better on ridged-up rows or raised beds. It is one of the few plants that will thrive in the South when planted among stepping stones that absorb and radiate a lot of heat.

Pulmonaria, lungwort (*Pulmonaria* sp.)

Perennial; hardiness zones 4–9, heat-zones 9–1
Mature height: 6 to 12 inches
Light to moderate shade

One of the earliest perennials to bloom, pulmonaria makes a good companion for native woodland wildflowers. Its leaves have a fancied resemblance to lungs, thus the name. You will like the overlay of silver on leaves, which looks like it was either airbrushed or dripped on, a la Jackson Pollock. The blossoms come in short, curving sprays, and in pink, blue, or purple, and the foliage on certain cultivars has wavy edges. The pulmonarias look best en masse, planted in drifts, and flower more reliably in light shade than in dark corners. Even though you will love the floral effect of pulmonaria, its real strength is its durable, light-colored foliage that brightens shaded spots all summer long.

Purple creeper, purple heart *(Tradescantia pallida* 'Purpurea', formerly *Setcreasea pallida)*

Semi-hardy perennial, usually lives over
    winter in zone 8b and further south;
    heat-zones 12–1

Mature height: 12 to 14 inches

Full sun to light shade, grows well in
    containers

Purple heart (*Tradescantia pallida*) at North Augusta, South Carolina

When you see a single purple creeper
plant, it doesn't make much of an impression. It
looks like a houseplant and, indeed, is grown as such
further north. But set out a bunch of plants close together as a groundcover and they create a stunning impact,
loved by some, strongly disliked by others. The long,
slender, fleshy leaves are shaped like canoes, each with a
cross section like a vee. Tiny, light colored flowers come in midsummer, but it is the shades of dark purple and pink in the leaves that
catch your eye. The plants grow short branches that root at the
nodes. The further south you go, the better purple creeper grows—
it thrives on heat and humidity and can survive the occasional dry
spell without losing its leaves. I've seen it growing happily in sandy
soil and in clay when given good drainage. Plants die back during the
winter but in the Lower South will regrow when warm weather
returns.

Purslane *(Portulaca umbraticola)*

Perennial; hardiness zones 7–9, but usually
    grown as an annual; heat-zones 9–7

Mature height: 2 to 4 inches

Full sun

The only thing this little beauty has in
common with the garden weed purslane is
the common name. It resembles more
closely portulaca or rose moss, and ranks
right up there with lantana for resistance to
heat. It has large, translucent single flowers, and
fleshy stems and leaves that are larger and fatter than
those of rose moss. Bodger Botanicals developed the
variety 'Hotshot' and has released a series of vegetatively-
propagated colors including some peachy-pink, coral, and

Flowering purslane (*Portulaca umbraticola* 'Yubi'), Park Seed Co. trials

apricot shades. They grow into low, moderately spreading plants that bloom only when the sun is out, not on dark days or at dawn or dusk. The 'Yubi' color series is also highly rated. Purslane likes to be grown on the dry side and will die in soggy soil. It will thrive in well-drained containers with a mulch of pebbles or sand. Toward the end of the summer purslane can wear out, exhausted from flowering and setting seeds. The volunteers that come up from them may not have the flower size and color range of the original plants. Pinch out branch tips if you want bushier plants.

Red hot poker (*Kniphofia uvaria*)

Perennial; hardiness zones 6–9, heat-zones 9–6
Mature height: 3 to 5 feet, depending on the culture
Full sun

Old clumps of red hot poker (*Kniphofia uvaria*) develop tall flowering stalks.

Red hot poker is no quiet, demure flower. The colors in the old-fashioned tall variety practically shout for attention, with spikes of golden yellow, topped with orange and scarlet. I have an old plant cheek by jowl with a southern magnolia, where its shoulder-high spikes show off against the dark green magnolia foliage. Every year the clump of grasslike leaves grows larger and generates more bloom spikes. Hummingbirds are drawn to its slim, descending, tubular blossoms. My plant needed two years to gather enough strength to begin blooming. Not so with the 1999 All-America Selections winner 'Flamenco', which will flower the first year if purchased as a gallon-size plant. It comes in yellow, orange, and red colors, and flowers at a height of 2½ feet. Also, the German wholesale seed company Benary has produced a range of softer colors in a short-plant kniphofia. Caution—red hot poker is a dryland plant that demands excellent drainage.

Rosemary (*Rosmarinus officinalis*)

Evergreen perennial, marginally hardy in zone 6; officially hardiness zone adaptability is 8–10, heat-zones 10–1
Mature height: 1 to 5 feet, depending on the cultivar
Full sun, excellent drainage

Rosemary deserves to be planted as an ornamental as well as a culinary herb. It blooms heavily during fall and winter, and bees depend on it for nectar and pollen during warm days. Plant growth habit varies from sprawling and trailing through mound-shaped and erect, depending on the cultivar. I have found the erect cultivar 'Tuscan Blue' to be the most hardy in my zone 7 garden. However, by packing stones the size of soccer balls around a usually tender creeping type of rosemary, I have brought it through several winters. I don't know why it works, but it does. You can buy cultivars with blue, pink, or deep lavender blossoms, but the foliage is the principal attraction. In very humid areas you may have to spray rosemary with a fungicide during the dog days of summer to keep it from melting out from foliar fungal diseases. Rosemary is also susceptible to nematode damage, which can be minimized by working organic matter into the soil before planting, or inoculating the soil with beneficial nematodes. Considering the heat resistance of rosemary it would seem a cinch to grow in the Deep South, but the humidity often does it in, and it has to be replanted. Also, rosemary is an evergreen plant and continues to grow if winter weather is sufficiently warm, but drastic drops in temperature can (and often do) damage or kill it.

Trailing or creeping rosemary (*Rosmarinus officinalis*) at Ohinitahe Estate, near Christchurch, New Zealand

Salvia (*Salvia* sp.)

> Perennial. Most species: hardiness zones 8–10, with heat-zone adaptability of 10–1. Some salvias, such as *S. guaranitica, S. koyame, S. lyrata,* and *S. madrensis,* need the summer warmth of heat-zones 10–8
> Mature height: 2 to 4 feet
> Full sun

I am convinced that, as a class, the salvias hold greater potential for southern gardens than any other genus of plants. You have only to wander through a perennial nursery to see my point. In recent years, several cultivars of salvia from numerous species have rocketed to popularity. Many of these wildflowers were saved from extinction in Mexico and Central America by a botanist,

Tropical salvia (*Salvia coccinea*) in Wilson garden

Blue salvia (*Salvia farinacea* 'Strata'), an All-America Selections award winner

Blue salvia (*S. farinacea* 'Victoria')

Sapphire sage (*S. guaranitica*) in Wilson garden

Richard Dufresne, and brought with them sturdy constitutions and tolerance for weather stresses. Their tubular flowers attract hummingbirds, butterflies, and bees. My favorites are sapphire sage (*S. guaranitica*) a long-blooming, purple-flowered species; Texas or autumn sage (*S. greggii*) a shrubby, bush-forming salvia that comes in several colors; and *S. madrensis*, a gorgeous yellow-flowered species with long spikes that color up late in the season. The Gulf Coast native, *S. coccinea*, produced the All-America Selections winner 'Lady in Red', which, for me, acts as a reseeding annual. By far the most popular is the versatile blue or mealycup sage (*S. farinacea*) which is grown as an annual in zones 6 and 7. The salvia best known in the North, *S. splendens*, tends to scorch or burn out in the South without afternoon shade. I haven't noticed any deer damage on blue salvia. Now, having said that, I have to brace myself for a torrent of reports to the contrary! (See the separate listing for Mexican bush salvia.)

Sedum (*Hylotelephium* sp., formerly *Sedum*)

    Perennials; hardiness zones 4–9, heat-zones 9–1

    Height: 8 inches to 2½ feet, depending on the cultivar

    Full sun or light shade

Of the many species of *Sedum*, the showy autumn sedum (*H. spectabile*) is probably the most popular. It is the one with fleshy foliage on erect plants that are topped with flattened blossom clusters. The blooms and foliage turn from light green to pink to purple as fall approaches. Butterflies come to the blossoms in droves. Also popular are the smaller cultivars with dark purple foliage, and the even smaller creeping type with variegated pink and white foliage. I also grow *H. ternatum*, a native from the Blue Ridge Mountains. All sedums grow best in zone eight and further north; the humidity further south is hard on them. Sedums grow best in well-drained soil. Unfortunately, the sedums are relished by deer and, in my garden, are among the first plants to be eaten by them during dry spells.

Ice plant sedum (*Hylotelephium spectabile* 'Autumn Glory') at Callaway Gardens, Pine Mountain, Georgia

Sky flower (*Duranta repens*)

Woody shrub, marginally hardy in zone 9; heat-zones 12–7
Mature height: 4–6 feet, but depends on the severity of winter
Full sun

When I first saw sky flower at a nursery, I rushed inside to ask the name of "that beautiful sky-blue shrub." They knew exactly which shrub I was excited over because it elicits the same response from many gardeners in zone 8 and further north. Further south, they are more accustomed to its beauty. In midsummer, open sprays of mid-blue blossoms that look a bit like crape myrtle begin a show that lasts all summer, and are followed by golden berries. The blossoms are out on the tips of branches, where they are very showy. The foliage is long and slender, a dusty light green in color. Sky flower also comes in a white-flowered selection, and one with variegated foliage. In zone 9 the shrubs may die to near the ground during severe winters but, if mulched deeply with pinestraw, should survive.

Sky flower (*Duranta repens*), a tropical shrub grown as an annual in hardiness zones 6, 7, and 8
PLANT PICS

Society garlic (*Tulbaghia violacea*) can add height to container plantings.

Society garlic (*Tulbaghia violacea*)

Perennial; hardiness zones 7–10, heat-zones 10–7
Mature height: 2½ feet to top of blossom clusters
Full sun or afternoon shade

This little ornamental would not amount to a blip on the popularity screen were it not for its adaptability to containers. Given the good drainage, and even occasional dryness of containers, the plants will bloom throughout the summer, with lemon-sized clusters of pink flowers. The variegated cultivar, with cream-colored margins on the grasslike leaves, is more popular than the pure green original. Society garlic is valued for its fountainlike growth and tall stems that add height to container plantings. It is often planted in herb gardens, on sandy mounds or among stones, where its continuous flowering brightens up the prevailing green or gray of herb foliage. In zones 6 and 7, dig the small bulbs, let them dry, and store them indoors during the winter, rather than letting them perish by freezing.

Spider lily (*Hymenocallis* sp., *Lycoris radiata*)

Hymenocallis: hardiness zones 8–11, heat-zones 12–8. *L. radiata*:
hardiness zones 8–10, heat-zones 10–7
Mature height: to 3 feet for *Hymenocallis* cultivars, 2 feet for *Lycoris*
Full sun or light shade

Several entirely different plants are commonly known as spider lilies. Two of the best for the South are the aquatic *Hymenocallis* species and *L. radiata*, which has many other fanciful names: hurricane lily, rain lily, surprise lily, etc., etc. *Hymenocallis* is a large, fleshy plant with long, slender leaves and curious pure white blossoms on thick, leafless stems. Its flaring blossoms are entire in the throat, but divide into slender, spidery segments near the tips. The stamens don't arise from the throat of the blossom, but from well out on the petals. *Hymenocallis* is best suited for growing on the banks of streams or ponds, but will also grow well in moist garden soil if it

Spider lily (*Hymenocallis* sp.) growing in a submerged pot at the Atlanta Botanical Garden

has a high water table. *L. radiata* goes through two distinct growth and development cycles, vegetative and flowering. The short, slender, dark green leaves die down in the summer, and the bare flowering stalks pop up later, usually after rain in August. Its red petals are narrow and curved back, which makes the blossom cluster take on a ball shape. *Lycoris* bulbs don't like to be disturbed. Neither genus is in color all summer but both are so interesting in their bloom and growth habit that they deserve a place in the garden. When you plant *L. radiata*, mix in a few bulbs of the diminutive copper lily (*Habranthus tubispathus* var. *texensis*) for yellow-orange blossoms to set off the color of the rain lilies.

Star cluster flower, pentas (*Pentas lanceolata*)

Semi-hardy perennial; hardiness zone 9 and further south; heat-zones
   12–1; grown as an annual further north
Mature height: 1 to 3 feet, depending on the variety
Full sun or light shade

If you haven't grown pentas, write in your garden journal, "Plant pentas next spring!" During the past decade pentas have sprinted from nowhere to near the top of the pack of summer flowers. In all probability, the rage for butterfly flowers helped, but the beauty and durability of pentas in all sorts of weather decided the race. Standard pentas grow up to three feet in height in rich soil, with dark green, furry, furrowed leaves on erect plants. I have a photo of me taken in Encinitas, California, with pentas taller than my head! Colors include dark red, purple, lavender, pink, and white. You can buy plants of a very compact cultivar that grow to only about half the height of standard pentas. Unfortunately, plant labels occasionally omit the mature height of the plant and you could end up with a duke's mixture of plant heights if you don't ask questions of the dealer. Whatever the height, your pentas will attract butterflies of all species, including the big guys who like to perch on the large clusters of tiny, star-shaped blossoms to extract nectar.

**Star cluster flower
(*Pentas lanceolata*)**

Stokes' aster (*Stokesia laevis*)

Perennial; hardiness zones 5–9, heat-zones 9–1

Mature height: to 2 feet

Full sun to light shade

Native to many southern states, Stokes' aster makes a handsome flowering perennial for borders. I've seen it blooming in February at Crosby Gardens in Picayune, Mississippi, but it doesn't flower until early summer in my zone 7 garden. The plants form heavy rosettes of long, thick, oval leaves. From these clumps arise tall, nearly leafless stems surmounted with many-petalled, lavender-purple flowers, often described as "blue." The plants bloom through much of the summer except when stressed by drought. Pink or white-flowered sports (color mutants) occasionally show up in wild populations, and have been increased for sale. Old clumps of Stokes' aster benefit from being divided every three or four years. Grow it with *Penstemon smallii* for a pleasing pink-and-blue combination.

A creamy white selection from the wild lavender-purple Stokes' aster (*Stokesia laevis*)

Sunflower (annual) (*Helianthus annuus*)

Annual, adapted throughout the south; heat-zones 12–1

Mature height: 3 to 15 feet, depending on the variety

Full sun

Flower arrangers and commercial florists, as well as butterfly and wild-bird fanciers, have pushed annual sunflowers into the limelight. Once prized for their gigantic plants and huge heads full of seeds prized by birds, sunflower plants have been downsized and a wide range of blossom colors and bicolors have been developed. You can still buy mammoth sunflowers to start children gardening, but the new emphasis is on plants more in scale with landscapes. But even the dwarf varieties, topping off at three feet in height, have to be placed toward the back of borders because their foliage is large, rough, and unfinished looking. The most popu-

Annual sunflower (*Helianthus annuus* 'Sunbright')

lar varieties grow to a height of four to six feet, and can produce long stems for cutting. Colors include not only sunflower yellow, but creamy white, mahogany red, brown, and gold. Blossoms range from three to six inches in diameter for the varieties bred for cutting. Sunflowers pull a lot of water out of the soil and tend to stress smaller flowers grown close to them. Literature says they are allelopathic, which means they can harm or kill plants growing around them (as walnut trees do with the toxic juglone produced by their roots), but I've not seen it happen in gardens.

Swan River daisy (*Brachycome iberidifolia*) Sometimes spelled *Brachyscome*.

> Perennial, usually grown as an annual; hardiness zones 9–10, heat-
> zones 12–1
> Mature height: 9 to 12 inches
> Full sun

Here is a worthy companion to Dahlberg daisies, a bit taller, and delivering pink, white, and violet-blue colors. An Australian native, Swan River daisy grows best in a dry environment. The fine-leafed plants look fragile but are far from it, holding up well in hot weather. Use the loosely mounded plants in edgings or containers as filler flowers. The daisy flowers are small, around one inch in diameter, but are abundant and long lasting. The plants are self-covering and overgrow spent blossoms, maintaining a neat look. The German seed company Benary is busy increasing the range of colors of this versatile little flower for use, I would assume, in the many planter boxes you see on the Continent and in containers over here.

Sweet potato (ornamental) (*Ipomoea batatas*)

> Tropical perennial, grown as an annual; heat-zones
> 12–1
> Runner length at maturity: 3 to 6 feet
> Full sun, away from strong wind

Ornamental sweet potatoes have gained popularity rapidly as their great performance in large containers has been recognized. Starting with a small plant in a six-inch pot, you can grow a plant with three

Tricolor sweet potato (*Ipomoea batatas*) in a container in the Wilson garden

or four long, trailing stems in only a month or two. Sweet potatoes need frequent watering in containers; their large, variously lobed leaves transpire a lot. And they need either controlled release fertilizer or liquid feeding every two weeks to keep them thriving. You can find plants with chocolate-colored, chartreuse, or tricolor (pink, cream, and white) foliage. Grow them just for foliage; sweet potatoes rarely bloom at our latitudes. Several plant breeders have been working on sweet potatoes and each has appended his own fanciful name to his particular color series, so just select the color you want and don't worry about the cultivar name. You will need to control snails, slugs, and earwigs to avoid getting unsightly holes in the foliage. When you grow them in large hanging baskets, you will minimize problems with such crawling mollusks and insects. Take cuttings in late autumn, root them in water, and pot them up to use as starter plants the following spring.

Torenia, wishbone flower (*Torenia fournieri*)

Tender perennial, mostly grown as an annual; hardiness zone 11, heat-zones 12–1

Mature height: 16 to 24 inches, depending on length of season

Light to moderate shade

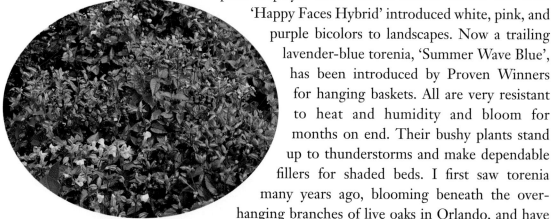

Wishbone flower (*Torenia fournieri* 'Clown Mixed Colors')

For many years, only blue torenia could be found in bedding plant displays. Then 'Clown Mixed Colors' and later 'Happy Faces Hybrid' introduced white, pink, and purple bicolors to landscapes. Now a trailing lavender-blue torenia, 'Summer Wave Blue', has been introduced by Proven Winners for hanging baskets. All are very resistant to heat and humidity and bloom for months on end. Their bushy plants stand up to thunderstorms and make dependable fillers for shaded beds. I first saw torenia many years ago, blooming beneath the overhanging branches of live oaks in Orlando, and have watched them gain steadily in favor across the South. The common name comes from the wishbone shape formed by the stamens in some blossoms. The modern varieties hold their flowers above the foliage rather than hiding them among the leaves.

Turk's cap, Mexican Turk's cap (*Malvaviscus arboreus* 'Mexicanus')

Semi-hardy perennial, usually grown as a reseeding annual; hardy
    through zone 9, heat-zones 12–8

Mature height: 3 to 5 feet, more in rich soil

Light shade

A rough, tough customer, Turk's cap can survive for decades
around abandoned farmsteads, renewing itself by dropping seeds.
The large, coarse foliage and awkward plants won't take any beauty
contests, but the dangling, dark red, turban-shaped blossoms and the
hummingbirds they attract are sufficient reason for planting it.
Native to South Florida, Mexico, and the Caribbean, Turk's cap will
shrug off extreme heat and humidity. Blooms form all summer long
and are followed by small, round fruits that birds distribute along
fence rows. Treat Turk's cap as an annual in hardiness zone 10 and
further north.

Tweedia (*Tweedia caerulea*)

Semi-hardy perennial; hardiness zone 10 and further south; heat-
    zones 12–8

Mature height: 2 to 2½ feet

Full sun

I wish this plant had a common name as
irresistible at its blue color. I've seen only
two other species that come close to
matching its ice-blue petals: Virginia bluebells and a *Phacelia*, native to California.
The plants also won't win any beauty contests, with their small, fleshy, narrow
leaves, and rather gawky form. But wow!
The blossoms! They aren't large, less than two
inches across, but their blue color is so incredible
that visitors will zoom in on it as soon as they enter your
garden. The flower buds are bicolored pink and blue. As
the stiff petals age they take on a pinkish cast. "Are they
real?" is a common question. I've grown tweedia as an
annual from plants I brought back from a visit to
Orlando. You may have to ask your garden center to order plants for
you, or you can order seeds from Thompson & Morgan. If you cut
the stems for arrangements, sear the cut ends to keep the milky juice
from bleeding.

**Blue-flowered
milkweed (*Tweedia
caerulea*)
Fearrington Resort,
North Carolina**

Verbena (perennial) (Hybrids between various species of *Verbena*)

Perennial; hardiness zones 9–11, heat-zones 12–4

Spreading plants, mature height: 1 foot, spread to 6 feet on older
plants

Full sun

The recently introduced perennial verbenas are neck and neck
with the perennial salvias for popularity. Some are selections from
the native *V. canadensis*, other hybrids may have blood
(genes) from *V. rigida* and *V. tenuisecta*. They
bloom for months at a time. I have seen verbena 'Homestead' begin blooming before any
other flower in a landscape (except spring
bulbs), and continue without pause until
just before Thanksgiving. That's about
eight months of color! 'Homestead', with
vibrant purple blossoms on spreading
plants, was the first of the series to be marketed. The lavender 'Abbeville', possibly another
accidental hybrid between two species growing
along roadsides, soon followed. Then a number of breeders jumped in to produce a slew of cultivars, including the
two popular color series, 'Tapien' and 'Temari'. The species
V. tenuifolia, or fern-leafed verbena, is favored for containers because it does not spread as rampantly as the larger-
leafed verbenas. A tall species, Argentine verbena (*V. bonariensis*) is
beloved by flower arrangers for its long, wiry stems, and by butterfly
fanciers, but it has escaped into farmlands and wild areas and threat-
ens to become a pestiferous weed. I dislike damning any flower with
faint praise, but I can't include the annual verbenas in my list of flowers for the South. They are beautiful, but grow much better in zone
6 and further north than under our hot, humid conditions.

Verbena
'Sissinghurst'.
Photo courtesy
of Park Seed
Co.

Veronica, speedwell (*Veronica spicata*)

Perennial; hardiness zones 3-8, but short-lived in zones 9 and 10;
heat-zones 8–1

Mature height: to 18 inches

Full sun or light shade

The most widely adapted veronica is 'Sunny Border Blue', a
cultivar with a fascinating history. Introduced many years ago, it
gradually lost out in the market and virtually disappeared. But a plant

expert came upon a survivor in a garden and tried it in the South, where it excelled. It was increased and reintroduced many years later. 'Sunny Border Blue' may not have originally come from the popular *V. spicata* as generally believed, but more closely resembles it than other species. In the South it produces erect plants with long, violet-blue spikes that hold their color a long time. If you deadhead the plants after the spikes have turned brown, feed and water them, and they will rebloom. You can recognize this cultivar by its crumpled, dark green leaves. If you want pink and white colors in veronica, you must turn to other *V. spicata* cultivars. None of them stand up to heat as well as 'Sunny Border Blue', except perhaps *V. longifolia*.

Veronica '**Sunny Border Blue**', **Wilson garden**

Vinca (big-leafed) (*Vinca major*)

Woody perennial vine; hardiness zones 7–11, heat-zones 12–7

Usually allowed to run on the ground or trail from hanging baskets

Full sun or light to moderate shade

I must begin this description with a caution. Don't plant the common green, big-leaf vinca near wildlands where it can spread. What was a small patch at the edge of a woodlot when we moved onto our farm has spread to cover an eighth of an acre, smothering all other forest-floor species in the process. I recommend you limit your purchases to the green-and-white variegated cultivar which isn't as rampant, and which trails nicely in containers, or go with the little-leaf species, *V. minor*, which spreads slowly. Variegated vinca is one of the most popular trailing plants for hanging baskets and for cascading over the edge of free-standing containers. Its woody vines hang as straight down as plumb bobs. It can tolerate extremes of heat, dryness, rain, and wind. Pests and plant diseases are few. Pretty blue flowers show in early spring but the evergreen foliage is the real draw for vinca vine.

Wild or summer petunia (*Ruellia brittoniana*)

Semi-hardy perennial, may survive winters in zone 10; heat-zones

12–7

Mature height: 16 to 24 inches

Afternoon shade

The ruellias are not petunias. The common name wild petunia comes from a fancied resemblance between the plants' blossoms. I

A southwestern wild petunia, *Ruellia brittoniana*, is winter hardy in zone 8 and south.

am accustomed to seeing native *R. caroliniensis* growing wild around my landscape. It was there when we moved in and comes back every year, but often in a different place. It is a winsome little lavender-flowered plant, but not particularly showy. However, selections from *R. brittoniana*, which is native to Mexico, are very showy and stand up well to heat and humidity. 'Katie' has short plants with long, narrow, dark green leaves, crowned with a cluster of deep purple blossoms. It makes a durable, beautiful plant for edging beds of taller flowers. 'Katie' performed well during a very hot summer but did not survive the winter in my garden. I first saw it at a national meeting of garden writers at San Antonio where a gaggle of our members were clustered around a bed of it, taking notes and photographs. The pink-flowered *R. brittoniana* cultivar 'Chi Chi' may be hardier than 'Katie'. Reportedly, it is hardy in zone 7 and possibly further north. You can mail-order purple, white, or pink colors of ruellia.

Wormwood, artemisia (*Artemisia* sp.)

Mostly woody perennials; hardiness zones 7–9, heat-zones 9–7
Mature height: to 2 feet
Full sun

Artemisia 'Powis Castle' at the Bishop's Garden, National Cathederal, Washington, DC

Artemisia 'Powis Castle' (possibly *A. arborescens*, *A. absinthium*) is one of the most popular silver-leaved plants in the United States. It, and many other bushy artemisias, such as 'Huntington', grow well in zone 8 and further north but can suffer from the extreme humidity further south. On a dry slope in my garden 'Powis Castle' has spread six feet wide, and I have to chop it back to keep it from smothering its neighbors. It spreads by rooting where stems touch the ground, not by underground runners like *A. ludoviciana* 'Silver King', and is easily controlled. 'Silver King' is a staple for making dried arrangements, wreaths, and swags, and can be discouraged from taking over a garden by hemming it in with edgings. Of the groundcover types, *A. stellerana* 'Silver

Brocade', native to the Atlantic coast, is the most tolerant of heat and humidity. It likes to be grown in gravel beds or sandy soils that dry off quickly after rains.

Yucca, bear grass, Adam's needle, Spanish dagger

(*Yucca flaccida*, formerly *Y. filamentosa*, and *Y. aloifolia*)

> *Y. flaccida*: perennial; hardiness zones 5–10, heat-zones 10–2
>
> *Y. aloifolia*: officially hardy only through zone 11, with a
> heat-zone range of 12–2
>
> Mature height of flowering stem: 4 feet in dry soil,
> higher in moist, fertile garden soil
>
> Full sun

The yuccas bloom for about a month in early summer, but the rosettes of dark green, stilletto-shaped leaves look good year-round. Many gardeners think of the yuccas as desert plants, but *Y. flaccida* is native to the humid Southeast as well as across to Texas. In my area it is often found growing in dense stands along abandoned railbeds. Apparently, yuccas like to root through the deep pile of stones into the soil beneath. Unlike Spanish dagger or Spanish bayonet (*Y. aloifolia*) which has stiff, wickedly pointed leaves, beargrass, or Adam's needle, forms a rosette of soft leaves that pose no danger to gardeners. The margins of its leaves are frayed, and fringed with soft curls of fibrous filaments. Some of the prettiest yuccas are found in the variegated selections such as 'Color Guard' (cream-and-green striped). Plant *Y. flaccida* in groups for a bold landscape accent. The tall spikes of ivory-white, pendent flowers stay in good condition for three to four weeks, depending on the temperature. In zone 9 and further south you may wish to try red yucca (*Hesperaloe parviflora*), a tender yucca look-alike with slender pink to red blossom spikes and very narrow, arching foliage. It is native to hot, dry areas of Texas and northern Mexico.

Variegated Adam's needle (*Yucca filamentosa* Color Guard')
PLANT PICS

Zinnia (narrow-leafed) (*Z. angustifolia*)

> Annual; heat-zones 12–1
>
> Mature height: to 2 feet
>
> Full sun with good air circulation

Like all garden zinnias, *Zinnia angustifolia* is native to Mexico. It stands up to heat and dryness much better than the large-flowered *Z. elegans* and is strongly resistant to powdery mildew, which is a

Narrow-leafed zinnia (*Z. angustifolia* 'Crystal White'), Park Seed Co. trials

scourge of most large-flowered types late in the season. It grows into dense plants about eighteen inches high and two feet across, larger in fertile soil. Early on, the plants of this species were rather sparsely flowered, but recently introduced selections have concentrated more flowers on smaller plants. They come in yellow, orange, or white blossom colors, all of which are single or double-flowered. The blossoms average 1½ inches in diameter. Park Seed Co. also offers the mildew-resistant 'Pinwheel Mix', with a broader range of colors and slightly larger flowers than those of *Z. angustifolia*.

Zinnia 'Profusion'

Annual in all zones; heat-zones 12–1
Mature height: 10 to 12 inches
Full sun, with good air circulation

A Japanese seed breeding company, Sakata Seed, has introduced two colors of this durable zinnia, 'Profusion Cherry' and 'Profusion Orange'. The series includes genes from *Z. angustifolia*, a Mexican zinnia with narrow leaves and high resistance to heat and to powdery mildew. The consistent excellence of 'Profusion' in U.S. and Canadian trials earned it a 1998 All-America Selections award. The dense, heavily branched plants of 'Profusion' spread to eighteen inches wide. Its semi-double flowers are medium sized, and spent blossoms are quickly hidden by new foliage. The extra layers of petals make the blossoms appear much fuller than those of *Z. angustifolia* culti-

Zinnia 'Profusion Cherry' All-America Selections Award winner

vars. 'Profusion' adapts well to growing in either ground beds or large containers where it has room to spread. If you use organic mulches in your landscape, keep them away from the base of these plants to avoid stem rot.

SIX

Flowers and Foliage Plants Recommended by Southern Experts

These lists may surprise and enlighten you. When I asked southern experts to prepare lists of flowers and foliage plants that grow well in their given areas, I stipulated that the plants recommended should provide continuous color from spring planting through fall frost. I sent inquiries to garden centers and botanical gardens as far west as Arkansas and East Texas, as far north as Virginia, and as far south as northern Florida. On the most recent version of the USDA Hardiness Zone Map, this area would include all or parts of zones 6 through 9b. I didn't include the Southwest because even though their summers can be intensely hot, humidity seldom causes problems. Also, they have to deal with alkaline soils and drying winds. By comparison, our soils tend to be acid, and our summer winds are usually associated with rainstorms. That's why you so seldom see windmills on southern farms; when they are needed to pump water, there isn't any wind to speak of.

Some of the species or cultivars recommended may be hard to find in reference books. Even my trusty old *Hortus Third* didn't describe some of them. *The Southern Living Garden Book* helped, as did the *RHS Dictionary of Garden Plants*. But the most help on names came from the experts whose recommendations will follow.

How, in this age of information, could a situation exist where so little is published about remarkably beautiful and durable flowers? It is due to their relative newness in the North American horticultural trade. Some kinds were imported recently from Australia and New Zealand, the South Pacific, South Africa, or little-known regions of Asia. Some tropical species may have been grown for years in South

Florida and the Caribbean but have only recently made their way northward to be grown as annuals. Some obscure hardy perennials are just now being evaluated for heat resistance in the South. Keep in mind that some plant genera are so diverse that while most of them may not be bulletproof under southern growing conditions, the cultivars of certain species may come through our summers with flying colors.

Your first reaction, when reading these reports from the field, will probably be to turn to a report from your immediate geographic area. Fine, but remember that any plant recommended in any of these lists should perform pretty well over much of the South. Just keep in mind that in hardiness zones eight though ten, many semi-tropical and some tropical species will live through their mild winters. That usually means bigger plants, because they will start the second and succeeding years' growth from established rootstocks, and will absorb more heat units during their long, hot growing season. With tropical species, the more heat they receive (consistent with sufficient humidity), the faster and larger they grow. That isn't the case with hardy perennials originally from cool areas of the world. Prolonged heat, and especially hot nights, can cause them to become stunted and perhaps to die.

When these reports began coming in, I found myself eagerly anticipating the surprises they contained. I wasn't disappointed, and I trust you will learn and benefit from them, too. The botanical names for certain species may not agree with those on the list of my favorite plants because not everyone wants to go along with some of the most radical taxonomic changes. I had to force myself, for example, to use the name *Solenostemon* in place of good old *Coleus*! I finally did, but it pains me.

Southern Perennials and Herbs

This list of flowers and foliage plants with exceptional resistance to heat and humidity was prepared by Barbara Bridges of Southern Perennials and Herbs in Tylertown, Mississippi, which is USDA hardiness zone 8b.

Botanical Name	Common Name
Abelmoschus manihot	Yellow abelmoschus
Abutilon × *hybridum*	Flowering maple cultivars

Alpinia nutans (A. zerumbet)	Ginger lily
Alternanthera ficoidea 'Bettzickiana'	Calico plant
Caryopteris × *clandonensis*	Bluebeard
Cestrum nocturnum 'Orange Peel' and 'Lemon Peel'	Hybrid shrub jessamine
Coreopsis integrifolia	Chipola River daisy
Crocosmia × *crocosmiiflora*	Montbretia
Cuphea ignea 'David Verity'	Orange firecracker flower
Cuphea sp. 'Flamingo Pink'	Pink firecracker flower
Dicliptera suberecta	Orange dicliptera
Duranta erecta (D. repens)	Sky flower
Elettaria cardamomum, 'Dwarf'	Dwarf cardamom (fragrant foliage)
Erigeron 'Profusion'	Daisy fleabane
Erythrina crista-galli	Crybaby tree (thorny)
Eupatorium fistulosum	Joe-Pye weed
Gaura lindheimeri	White gaura
Hedychium species such as: H. *angustifolium* (peach) H. *coccineum* H. *coronarium* H. *gardnerianum* H. *gracile*	All of these are flowering gingers and are hardy here. They have good, tropical-looking foliage and beautiful flowers in late summer.*
Hemerocallis spp.	Daylily cultivars
Hibiscus grandiflorus	Great rose mallow
Hibiscus moscheutus 'Dixie Belle Mixed Colors', 'Doogie's Rose', 'Southern Belle Mixed Colors', et. al.	Large-flowered hardy hibiscus cultivars
Hibiscus mutabilis	Confederate rose mallow (also known as Confederate rose)

Iris, Louisiana Hybrids	Complex hybrids developed from native southeastern species
Iris xiphium	Spanish iris
Kaempferia spp.:	Peacock gingers*
K. galanga	
K. gilbertii	
K. laotica	
K. pulchra	
K. rotunda	Resurrection lily, tropical crocus

* Ms. Bridges made an excellent suggestion regarding the dwarf cultivars of flowering gingers, ginger lilies, and the peacock gingers. She says that, in their climate zone, they make good substitutes for hostas. (In Tylertown, only a few cultivars of hostas do well.)

Lespedeza thunbergii	Bush lespedeza
Leucanthemum vulgare 'May Queen'	Oxeye daisy
Liatris microcephala	Littlehead liatris
Linernia floribunda	No common name
Malvaviscus arboreus 'Drummondii' and *M. a.* 'Mexicanus'	Turk's cap Mexican Turk's cap
Mirabilis jalapa	Four o'clock
Oenanthe javanica 'Flamingo'	Flamingo thing
Patrinia scabiosifolia 'Nagoya'	Yellow patrinia
Patrinia villosa	White patrinia
Pavonia braziliensis	Pink Brazilian pavonia

Salvia spp. My favorites are winter hardy species and cultivars of:

S. glechomifolia	
S. guaranitica	
S. greggi cultivars	Autumn sage
S. leucantha	Mexican bush salvia
S. lyrata	Lyre-leafed sage
S. madrensis	
S. uliginosa	

Scutellaria spp.	Skullcap
Sedum 'Autumn Joy', 'Brilliant', 'Meteor', and 'Carmen'	*Sedum spectabile* and showy stonecrop
Silphium gracile	Rosinweed
Solanum pseudocapsicum	Jerusalem cherry
Stokesia laevis	Stokes' aster
Talinum paniculatum	Jewels of Opar
Thunbergia battescombei	Blue thunbergia
Tibouchina urvilleana	Glory bush
Veronica 'Blue Charm', 'Sunny Border Blue'	Speedwell
Vernonia altissima	Ironweed
Vinca major 'Variegata'	Variegated bigleaf periwinkle

Roy Wyatt

Shortly before his death in 1998, Roy Wyatt, a friend of many years, longtime Garden Editor of the *Atlanta Journal-Constitution*, and a past president of the Garden Writers Association of America, contributed this list of flowers that can take the heat in his hardiness zone 7 area of Alpharetta, Georgia.

Botanical Name	**Common Name**
ANNUALS	
Alternanthera ficoides	Joseph's coat
Catharanthus roseus	Periwinkle (erroneously called "vinca")
Cleome hassleriana	Spider flower
Cosmos sulphureus	Yellow or orange cosmos
Gomphrena globosa	Globe amaranth
Impatiens, New Guinea hybrids	New Guinea impatiens
Melampodium paludosum	Butter daisy

Mirabilis jalapa	Four o'clock
Perilla frutescens	Beefsteak plant
Petunia 'Purple Wave' and 'Pink Wave'	'Wave' petunias
Portulaca grandiflora	Rose moss
Scabiosa caucasica	Pincushion flower
Senecio cineraria and *Artemisia stellarana*	Dusty miller
Tagetes erecta and triploids of *T. patula*	Marigold, African and triploids
Tradescantia pallida (*Setcreasea pallida*)	Purple creeper, purple heart, setcreasea
Zinnia angustifolia	Narrow-leaved zinnia

PERENNIALS

Achillea millefolium	Milfoil
Artemisia spp.	Wormwood and Southernwood
Asclepias tuberosa	Butterfly weed
Delosperma cooperi	Hardy ice plant
Echeveria spp.	Hen and chicks
Echinacea purpurea	Purple coneflower
Gaillardia spp.	Indian blanket and blanket flower
Hemerocallis spp.	Daylily cultivars
Liorope muscari	Lily turf (this one forms clumps)
Liriope spicata	Liriope, creeping lily turf
Perovskia atriplicifolia	Russian sage
Phlox subulata	Thrift (also used for *Armeria*)
Platycodon sp.	Balloon flower

Rudbeckia sp.	Black-eyed Susan
Salvia leucantha	Mexican bush salvia
Sedum spectabile cultivars	Autumn sedum
Verbena hybrids such as 'Homestead'	Perennial verbena
Veronica cultivars	Speedwell

Roy Wyatt added that although most of these flowers will withstand drought pretty well, all will do better if watered weekly during dry spells, especially New Guinea impatiens and melampodium.

Zimlich's Patio and Garden Center

Zimlich's Patio and Garden Center has served the coastal Alabama area for three generations. Tommy and Donald Zimlich prefaced their recommendations with these words of advice:

"We are glad to share what we know about Gulf Coast gardening. The peculiarities of the climate right on the coast are seldom considered in national publications. Plants that grow well in Montgomery, or in towns as nearby as Brewton, Alabama, often do not fare well in Mobile.

"Our list divides plants into annuals or perennials, but these terms are often misleading in this area. Our winters are sometimes so mild that tropicals and plants considered annuals further north may overwinter. Many of our customers think of overwintering annuals as perennials, but we feel they are stretching the definition of 'perennials.'

"This is a core list. We grow and experiment with other plants but those on this list survive the retail market year after year."

Adapted Annuals and Tender Perennials Grown as Annuals

Angelonia salicariifolia 'Hilo Princess'*

Begonia semperflorens 'Cocktail' color series for sunny gardens, 'Olympia' for shade

Caladiums for beds or containers receiving light to moderate shade: 'Candidum', Gingerland', 'Miss Muffet', and 'Red Flash'

Coreopsis grandiflora 'New Gold' and 'Sunray', full sun

Coleus, sun-tolerant 'Alabama', and 'Brandy', full sun to light shade

Evolvulus glomeratus subsp. *grandiflorus* 'Blue Daze'*

Lantana (These often regrow after mild winters.) 'New Gold', 'Irene', 'Confetti', and 'Dallas Red'; full sun to light shade

Impatiens, standard varieties. These look great in lightly shaded beds, especially when combined with caladiums. Try to match the blossom colors of the impatiens with the vein color of the caladiums for a spectacular effect. We like:

'Accent Coral' impatiens with 'Miss Muffet' caladiums

'Accent Red' impatiens with 'Red Flash' caladiums

'Accent White' impatiens with 'Candidum' caladiums

'Accent Apricot' impatiens with 'Gingerland' caladiums

Impatiens, New Guinea hybrids. Grow them in light to moderate shade.

Mexican heather *(Cuphea hyssopifolia)*. Loves hot sun and often overwinters here.

Periwinkle or Madagascar periwinkle *(Catharanthus roseus)*. These withstand heat but can develop root rot in poorly drained soil. The 'Little' color series grows ranker but is hardier than the newer 'Pacifica' and 'Tropicana' colors. Pull out periwinkle plants in the fall and plant dark-leafed begonias the following spring to discourage buildup of soil-borne diseases.

Rudbeckia 'Irish Eyes', 'Indian Summer', and 'Goldsturm'. Plant these cultivars in full sun.

Salvia coccinea (red) and blue salvia, *S. farinacea* 'Victoria Blue', also *S. splendens* 'Red Hot Sally'

Zinnia 'Dreamland' hybrid, quite resistant to leaf spot

Perennials

Allamanda†

Bougainvillea †

Copper Plant *(Acalypha)* †

Mandevilla (Dipladenia) †

Hibiscus, tropical †

Plumbago †

Petunia hybrids and new near-petunia species. 'SunVale', 'Pampas Fire', and 'Sun Wine'. Million Bells (*Calibrachoa*) 'Cherry Pink', 'Trailing Blue', and 'Pink' Supertunias. These bloom longer during hot weather than annual petunias.

Queen Anne's lace. We grow our plants from seeds harvested from wild stands near Noonan, Georgia, and they do great.

Verbena, hybrid, 'Temari' and 'Tapien' colors, and 'Homestead'; usually overwinter here.

* Both angelonia and evolvulus are blue flowers and grow well here. Few other blue flowers do well on the Coast. These two do best in full sun on well-drained soil. They could live through an exceptionally mild winter, but we grow them as annuals here.

† These and other tropicals from South Florida grow very well here in full sun or light shade, but we have to protect them during the winter or they will freeze to the ground.

Plantation Nursery Co.

Plantation Nursery Co. in Meridianville, Alabama, is about as far away from the Gulf Coast as you can go without crossing over into Tennessee. It lies northwest of metropolitan Huntsville, in the foothills leading up to the Cumberland Plateau. Its winters are short but sharp, and its summers long and often dry. Problems with humidity and hot nights are not as severe as in southern Alabama. The town is small enough that a letter I sent without a street address was delivered promptly to Thomas D. Batt, my contact at Plantation. Here's Tom's list of heat- and humidity-resistant plants.

Annuals or Tender Perennials Grown as Annuals

Coleus 'Wizard Mixed Colors'

Dianthus 'Telstar Mixed Colors'

Ageratum 'Blue Puffs'

Alyssum 'Rosie O' Day'*

Gaillardia grandiflora 'Goblin'

Iceland poppy, *Papaver nudicaule* 'Champagne Bubbles'*

Marigold, African, *Tagetes erecta* 'Inca Yellow'

Nicotiana 'Metro Mixed Colors'

Petunia 'Pink Wave' and 'Purple Wave'

Salvia 'Red Hot Sally'

Salvia farinacea 'Victoria Blue'

Wishbone flower, *Torenia fournieri* 'Clown Mixed Colors'

Hardy Perennials

Candytuft, perennial, *Iberis sempervirens* 'Purity'*

Coreopsis verticillata 'Zagreb'

Black-eyed Susan, *Rudbeckia hirta* 'Goldilocks' and 'Indian Summer'

Geum chiloense 'Lady Strathden'

Gaura lindheimeri 'Whirling Butterflies'

Helianthus helianthoides var. *scabra* 'Summer Sun'

Lavender, *Lavandula angustifolia* 'Munstead'

Lenten rose, *Helleborus orientalis*

Phlox paniculata 'Franz Schubert'

Purple coneflower, *Echinacea purpurea* 'Bravado'

Russian sage, *Perovskia atriplicifolia* 'Longin'

Salvia superba 'Blue Hill' and 'May Night'

Stachys byzantina 'Countess Helene von Stein' or 'Big Ears', a large-leafed lamb's ear

Veronica 'Goodness Grows'

Verbena canadensis hybrid 'Homestead Purple'

*Tom wanted these three flowers included in the list because they are such good performers in the spring and fall of the year. While they aren't especially resistant to heat and humidity, they make welcome additions to spring and fall landscapes.

Garden of Eden Nursery and Landscape

Hot Springs, Arkansas, home of famous spas, is also the home of Garden of Eden Nursery and Landscape. I contacted Harry and Kathy Childs, the owners, during their spring rush. Nevertheless, despite business being fast and furious, they found time to send a list of their best-selling heat- and humidity-resistant flowers:

Sun-Loving Annuals

Coleus, sun-tolerant, most cultivars, in particular 'Alabama Sunset'. These do well in full sun or light shade.

Begonia, wax-leafed 'Cocktail' series colors, especially the bronze-leafed, red-flowered 'Vodka' and the rose-pink–flowered, bronze-leafed 'Gin'

Mexican heather *(Cuphea hyssopifolia)*

Petunia, 'Purple Wave' and 'Pink Wave'

Sun-Loving Perennials

Coreopsis verticillata 'Moonbeam'

Lantana 'Gold Mound'; very heat resistant

Nierembergia 'Mont Blanc' (white). Often grown as an annual, this remarkably heat-resistant little flower will live through mild winters.

Shade-Loving Perennials

*Ligularia dentata** or bigleaf golden ray

*Author's note: *Ligularia dentata* is just becoming popular for shade gardens in the Midsouth. It has rather large, rounded leaves that can be green or purple, depending on the cultivar, and long, leafless, purple stems topped by large umbrellas of yellow-gold, daisylike flowers.

San Felasco Nurseries, Inc.

Gainesville, Florida, has a climate that allows gardeners to grow both northern and southern flowers. Most years, semi-tropical plants will survive their winters, and many hardy perennials will survive their summers. Except for occasional setbacks from blue northers that can blow in during late winter, many plants flourish year-round (including weeds). The climate provides an excellent proving ground for semi-tropical cultivars that have potential as annuals further north. San Felasco Nurseries, Inc. capitalizes on their climate to produce and ship many heat-resistant cultivars to retailers all over the Southeast. They also sell at retail through their garden center, The Plant Shoppe, in Gainesville.

Alan Shapiro of San Felasco sent me their wholesale list of eight hundred perennial cultivars and marked the ones that are notably resistant to heat and humidity. It follows. The helpful comments are his.

Botanical Name	Common Name
GROUNDCOVERS	
Ajuga reptans	Geneva bugleweed
A. reptans 'Burgundy Glow' (both bugleweeds bloom in the summer)	Tricolor bugleweed
Dietes bicolor	Yellow African iris
Dietes iridioides (Dietes vegeta)	White African iris
Hosta cultivars	
H. fortunei 'Aureo-marginata', 'Patriot', 'Francee', 'Frances Williams', 'Ginkgo Craig', 'Golden Tiara', 'Golden Standard'. *H. fortunei* hybrids 'August Moon', 'Honeybell', and 'Royal Standard'. *H. undulata* 'Albo-marginata' and 'Medio-variegata'. *H. ventricosa* 'Albo-marginata' and 'Wide Brim'.	
Wedelia trilobata (a constant-blooming groundcover)	No common name
VINES	
Antigonon leptopus	Coral vine
Aristolochia elegans (pretty, constant-blooming vine)	Dutchman's pipe, calico flower
Clytostoma callistegioides (sporadic bloomer here)	Purple painted trumpet vine
Jasminium sambac (constant bloomer, fragrant)	Indian jasmine

Lablab purpureus   Hyacinth bean vine
    (formerly *Dolichos lablab*)

Lonicera sempervirens   Red honeysuckle

Mandevilla sanderi (*Dipladenia sanderi*)   No common name
    (constant flowering; freezes here without protection)

Mandevilla splendens   No common name
    (freezes here, along with ixora, bougainvillea, and allamanda,
    but provides lots of warm-season color)

Podranea ricasoliana   Pink trumpet flower

Solanum jasminoides 'Variegata'   Variegated potato vine

Trachelospermum jasminoides   Confederate jasmine

FLOWERING HERBACEOUS PLANTS

Abutilon × *hybridum*   Parlor maple
    (freezes here but comes back from volunteer seedlings)

Achillea millefolium 'Summer Pastels'   Milfoil or yarrow

Agapanthus africanus   Lily of the Nile

Allium tuberosum   Garlic chives

Angelonia angustifolia   Angel plant
    (winter hardy, long-blooming)

Asclepias curassavica   Bloodflower
    (host plant for monarch butterfly larvae; constant bloom)

Asystasia gangetica   Ganges primrose
    (good flowering plant, but not cold-hardy here)

Barleria cristata   Philippine violet

Brugsmansia × *candida*   Angel's trumpet

Buddleia davidii 'Black Knight', 'Empire Blue',   Butterfly bush
    'Lavender', 'Lilac', 'Nanho Blue', 'Pink Delight', 'Purple',
    'Royal Red', 'White Profusion'

Buddleia sp. 'Lochinch'

Buddleia × *weyeriana*   Yellow butterfly bush

Calathea louisae   Hardy calathea

Canna × *generalis*	Canna lily

'Aida', 'Black Knight', 'Cleopatra', 'Journey's End', 'Pink Beauty', 'President', 'Richard Wallace', 'Rosemond Cole', 'Salmon Pink', 'Stadt Feltback', 'Striped Beauty', 'Wyoming', 'Yellow King Humbert'

Caryopteris × *clandonensis*	Blue mist shrub

'Dark Knight' and 'Longwood Blue'

Cassia corymbosa	Summer cassia

(hardier than most cassias and a constant bloomer)

Centratherum punctatum	Button flower

(*C. intermedium*)

Cestrum nocturnum	Night-blooming jasmine
Clerodendrum bungei	Pagoda plant, rose red

(invasive, but draws hummingbirds)

Clerodendrum paniculatum	Pagoda plant, orange-red
Clerodendrum speciossissimum	Red pagoda plant
Clerodendrum ugandense	Blue butterfly flower

(less hardy than other clerodendrums)

Coreopsis grandiflora 'Baby Sun', 'Early Sunrise'

Coreopsis lanceolata	Lance-leaved coreopsis
Coreopsis leavenworthii	Tickseed
Coreopsis rosea	Pink coreopsis
Coreopsis verticillata 'Moonbeam', 'Zagreb'	Threadleaf coreopsis
Crinum asiaticum	Crinum lily, white
Crocosmia spp. 'Ember Glow', 'Jupiter', 'Lucifer'	Montbretia
Crossandra infundibuliformis	Crossandra

(not winter-hardy here but lots of warm-season color)

Cuphea hyssopifolia	Mexican heather
Cuphea llavea	Georgia scarlet cuphea
Cuphea sp.	Allyson heather

Delosperma cooperi	Hardy iceplant
Dianthus gratianopolitanus 'Firewitch' (blooms better here than other perennial dianthus)	No common name
Echinacea purpurea	Coneflower, purple
Erigeron 'Profusion' (constant bloomer)	Midsummer aster
Euryops pectinatus (may freeze out and not regrow)	Silver-leafed bush daisy
Evolvulus glomeratus subsp. *grandiflorus*	Blue daze
Gaillardia grandiflora	Blanket flower
Gamolepis chrysanthemoides (may freeze out, but lots of warm-season color)	Bush daisy
Gaura lindheimeri 'Whirling Butterflies'	White gaura
Hamelia patens (a Florida native and constant bloomer)	Firebush
Hemerocallis	Daylily

These are the best repeat bloomers, but some of them will bloom more than others: 'Aztec Gold', 'Butterscotch Ruffles', 'Double Cutie', 'Irish Elf', 'Lil Business', 'Pojo', 'Tiny Pumpkin', 'Wilson's Yellow'.

Hibiscus coccineus	Red swamp mallow
H. grandiflorus	Great rose mallow
H. moscheutos	Rose mallow
H. mutabilis	Confederate rose
Hypoestes phyllostachya (doesn't bloom until fall, but the foliage color is the drawing card)	Polka dot plant
Justicia brandegeana	Shrimp plant
J. carnea	Jacobinia
J. ovata	Orange shrimp plant

Lantana camara	Bush lantana

'Confetti' pink & yellow, 'Delheim Pink', 'Fuchsia',
'Gold Mound', 'Horizon', 'Miss Huff', 'Red', 'Silver Mound',
'Tangerine', and 'Upright Yellow' (Lantana survives all but bad
winters here and provides constant bloom.)

L. montevidensis	Trailing lantana, purple or white
Lysimachia congestiflora (constant bloom)	Creeping Jenny
Malvaviscus arboreus 'Mexicanus'	Dwarf Turk's cap
Mirabilis jalapa (constant bloom)	Four o'clock
Odontonema strictum (attracts hummingbirds)	Firespike
Orthosiphon stamineus (not reliably winter-hardy here)	Cat's whiskers
Oxalis regnelli (O. triangularis)	Pink oxalis
Pentas lanceolata	Pentas, star cluster flower

(constant bloom if cold weather doesn't ruin it)

Perovskia atriplicifolia	Russian sage
Plumbago auriculata 'Blue' and 'Alba'; 'Imperial Blue' has the darkest flowers	Plumbago
Pseuderanthemum alatum	Chocolate soldiers, chocolate plant
Rudbeckia fulgida 'Goldsturm'	Black-eyed Susan
R. hirta 'Goldilocks', 'Indian Summer', 'Becky'	Black-eyed Susan
R. laciniata	Green eyes, cutleaf coneflower
Ruellia brittoniana 'Blue', 'Chichi',	Summer petunia

'Katie' (dwarf) (All of these ruellias are excellent bloomers.)

Salvia azurea 'Grandiflora' (Syn. *S. pitcheri*)	Azure sage
Salvia greggii	Autumn sage
S. guaranitica 'Argentine Sky', 'Purple Majesty'	Sapphire sage
Salvia 'Indigo Spires'	Perennial blue salvia
S. leucantha	Mexican bush salvia or Mexican sage
S. madrensis	Forsythia sage
S. miniata	Belize sage
Salvia × *superba* 'May Night'	Blue salvia
S. uliginosa	Bog sage
S. vanhoutteii	Burgundy sage
Saxifraga stolonifera	Strawberry geranium
Scutellaria 'Purple Fountain' (not reliably cold hardy here)	Skullcap
Sedum acre	Golden carpet sedum
Stachytarpheta jamaicensis (great butterfly plant)	Porter weed, blue
Stachytarpheta mutabilis (Neither of the porterweeds is cold hardy here.)	Porterweed, pink, and pink snake plant
Stokesia laevis	Stokes' aster
Tabernaemontana coronaria	Crape jasmine
Tibouchina urvilleana (*T. semidecandra*) 'Athens Blue'	Athens Blue tibouchina
Tradescantia pallida (Syn. *Setcreasea pallida*)	Purple heart, purple creeper, setcreasea
Tulbaghia violacea	Society garlic
Verbena bonariensis	Upright verbena
Verbena, named varieties selected for colors	Perennial verbena

V. tenuisecta	Perennial moss verbena
Verbena × *hybrida* 'Homestead Purple'	Purple verbena
Veronica longifolia 'Icicle'	White veronica
Veronica 'Goodness Grows', 'Sunny Border Blue'	Veronica
Viola floridana	Wild violet

ORNAMENTAL GRASSES

Cortaderia selloana	Pampas grass
Pennisetum alopecuroides	White fountain grass
Pennisetum alopecuroides 'Little Bunny'	Dwarf fountain grass
P. setaceum 'Burgundy Giant'	Burgundy giant fountain grass
P. setaceum 'Rubrum'	Red fountain grass

Note: San Felasco also offers other ornamental grasses: *Miscanthus, Muhlenbergia, Eragrostis,* et al.

FLOWERING GINGERS OF SEVERAL DIFFERENT SPECIES

Alpinia galanga	Thai spice ginger
Costus curvibracteatus	Orange tulip ginger
Costus spicatus	Spiral flag ginger
Curcuma sp.	Tulip ginger

(We sell several species or cultivars of tulip ginger. Their inflorescences last a long time. Some bloom in early summer, some later in the summer.)

Dichorisandra thyrsiflora	Blue ginger
Globba globulifera	Purple globe
Globba marantina (Syn. *G. schomburgkii*)	Dancing Girl ginger
Hedychium coronarium	Butterfly ginger
H. gardnerianum	Kahili ginger

H. greenei	Orange delta
H. hasseltii	Luna moth ginger
H. thyrsiforme	White pincushion
Kaempferia atrovirens	Silver spot peacock ginger
K. pulchra	Peacock ginger
Zingiber darceyi	Variegated pinecone ginger
Z. zerumbet	Red pinecone ginger

Flower Market, Inc.

Jeff Cooper at the Flower Market, Inc. sent a list of plants that in his Knoxville, Tennessee, hardiness zone 7a area can be counted on for at least eight weeks of summer color, either in landscapes or in containers. The Flower Market is a retail garden center and landscape nursery with many years' service to East Tennessee gardeners. Mary Spengler is the owner.

Botanical Name	**Common Name**
WINTER-HARDY PERENNIALS	
Coreopsis verticillata 'Moonbeam'	Threadleaf coreopsis
Echinacea purpurea 'Magnus'	Purple coneflower
Lavandula × *intermedia* 'Provence'	Hybrid lavender (lavandin)
Rosmarinus officinalis 'Arp'	Hardy rosemary
Salvia farinacea 'Victoria'	Blue salvia
Verbena bonariensis	Tall verbena
ANNUALS AND TENDER PERENNIALS	
Gomphrena globosa	Globe amaranth
Lantana × 'Confetti'	Hybrid lantana
Mandevilla xamoena 'Alice du Pont'	Mandevilla
Pentas lanceolata 'Pink Profusion'	Egyptian starflower
Petunia integrifolia	Creeping petunia

Plumbago auriculata	Cape plumbago
Verbena canadensis 'Rosea'	Trailing verbena

Dan West Garden Center

I lived for some years in Tennessee; in fact, I graduated high school in Memphis. Thus I knew that I needed lists of heat- and humidity-resistant flowers from West Tennessee as well as from Knoxville. The two climates are considerably different. Fred Heckle III at Dan West Garden Center in Memphis, for whom I have lectured in years past, sent a great list. Their store has been a mecca for gardeners for as long as I can remember.

Botanical Name	**Common Name**
Asteriscus maritimus 'Gold Coin'	Marguerite
Bacopa spp. 'Snowflake' and 'Mauve Mist'	Bacopa
Bidens ferulifolia 'Goldie' and 'Gold Marie'	Tickseed
Coreopsis verticillata 'Moonbeam' and 'Nana'	Threadleaf coreopsis
Cosmos sulphureus 'Bright Lights'	Gold and yellow cosmos
Dyssodia tenuiloba	Dahlberg daisy
Evolvulus glomeratus subsp. *grandiflorus* (syn. *E. nuttallianus*)	Blue daze
Gomphrena globosa	Globe amaranth
Helichrysum spp.	Strawflower
Lantana hybrids 'Confetti' and 'New Gold'	Lantana
Melampodium paludosum 'Medallion'	Melampodium
Nierembergia spp. 'Mont Blanc' and 'Violacea'	Cupflower
Pentas lanceolata, assorted colors	Egyptian star clusterflower

Petunia hybrids
    'Wave' color series
    'Supertunia' color series
	Petunias

Plumbago auriculata 'Royal Cape'	Cape plumbago

Rudbeckia hirta 'Indian Summer'	Black-eyed Susan
Salvia spp.and cultivars (grow as annuals here)	
Salvia coccinea 'Lady in Red'	Native Texas red salvia
S. farinacea 'Victoria' and 'Strata'	Blue salvia
Scaevola amoena 'Blue Wonder'	Fan flower
Torenia fournieri	Wishbone flower, blue wings

Verbena hybrids
   'Taipen' color series
   'Homestead Purple'
   'St. Paul'
   'St. Paul Red'
	Perennial verbena

Zinnia angustifolia (formerly *Z. linearis*)	Mexican zinnia

Riverbanks Zoo and Botanical Garden

One of the newest and most talked-about gardens in the Carolinas is the Riverbanks Zoo and Garden at Columbia, South Carolina. They do a great job of growing semi-tropical and tropical plants out-of-doors in a walled garden. Summers in Columbia's zone 8 climate are quite hot, but a bit less humid than down on the coast. Jim Martin of the Riverbanks Garden sent me this list. I was pleased to see (at last) a mention of one of my favorite flowers, Mexican poppy. But, alas, a later report from Jim added, "Mexican poppy is not looking so great right now. I think our clay soils and its location in our garden is having an effect on its progress."

Botanical Name	**Common Name**
Alternanthera dentata 'Rubiginosa' from Wave Hill Garden	No common name, grown for its purple foliage
Canna 'Bengal Tiger'	Striped canna
Cestrum parquii	Willow-leaved jessamine
Cuphea glutinosa	Mexican heather
Hamelia patens	Firebush (attracts hummingbirds)

Hunnemannia fumariifolia	Mexican poppy
Lantana trifolia	Shrub verbena
Salvia × 'Indigo Spires'	Blue salvia (one of many with this common name)
Scaevola aemula	Fan flower (requires a diligent watering schedule)
Turnera ulmifolia	Yellow sage rose
Veronica 'Sunny Border Blue'	Veronica

Lakewood Gardens

Over the years, I've lectured three times at Lakewood Gardens, North Little Rock, on behalf of Arkansas Public Television. They have a large and loyal clientele. Even though North Little Rock is nearly on line with Memphis, its climate is different, as are local tastes in flowers. Mike Wallis, a friend of several years, sent me this list along with a note: "Jim, here's a list of flowers that are good performers for summer color in our area. Not all of them will bloom all summer, but all have been dependable for us."

Botanical Name	**Common Name**
PERENNIALS	
Asclepias tuberosa	Butterfly weed
Canna cultivars, particularly the new dwarf types	Canna
Echinacea purpurea	Purple coneflower
Eupatorium fistulosum	Joe-Pye weed
Gaillardia grandiflora	Indian blanket
Helianthus multiflorus 'Loddon Gold'	Perennial sunflower
Monarda didyma 'Cambridge Scarlet'	Bee balm
Rudbeckia hirta 'Indian Summer'	Gloriosa daisy
Ruellia humilis	Wild petunia
Ruellia strepens	Wild petunia

ANNUALS

(those indicated as tropical are grown here as summer annuals)

Acalypha wilkesiana (tropical)	Copper leaf
Calandrinia umbellata	Rock purslane
Coleus, sun tolerant (tropical)	Sun coleus
Hamelia patens (tropical) (a wonderful hummingbird flower)	Firebush
Ixora 'Nora Grant' (tropical)	Florida honeysuckle
Lantana montevidensis (tropical)	Trailing lantana
Nierembergia hippomanica 'Mont Blanc'	Cup flower
Pentas lanceolata (tropical)	Star clusterflower
Plumbago auriculata (tropical)	Cape plumbago
Ruellia brittoniana 'Katie'	Dwarf ruellia
Ruellia malacosperma	Ruellia
Scaevola aemula	Fan flower

University of Tennessee

I was fortunate to receive two reports from Knoxville, Tennessee, including this one from Susan Wilson Hamilton, an assistant professor at University of Tennessee, listing the annuals that have performed best in their evaluation trials. These notes were taken after an exceptionally rainy summer which prompted Dr. Hamilton to remark, "It was a good growing season to evaluate resistance to root disease. Early on, it rained so much that, for the first time in seven years, we had to apply a soil fungicide to the garden to try to remedy the root rot. Drier weather in July and August helped, and our test garden ended up looking pretty good. We experienced more days than normal above 90°F in July and August, but the temperature rarely exceeded 95°."

(The symbol AAS means the variety recently received an All-America Selections award.)

Species Name	Common Name and Variety
ANNUALS	
Abelmoschus sp.	Abelmoschus 'Oriental' color series
Ageratum sp.	Ageratum 'Hawaii' series and 'Blue Blanket'
Begonia semperflorens	Begonia, wax-leafed, several color series: 'Varsity', 'Expresso', 'Rio', 'Vision', 'Atlanta', 'Victory', 'Alfa', and 'All-Round'
Capsicum frutescens	Ornamental pepper 'Red Missile'
Catharanthus rosea	Periwinkle or Madagascar periwinkle 'Blue Pearl'
Celosia plumosa	Celosia 'Prestige Scarlet' (AAS), 'Pink Castle' (AAS), 'New Look' (AAS), 'Sparkler', and 'Miss Nippon'
Celosia plumosa (Spicata group)	Wheat celosia 'Pink Candle' and 'Rose Tassels'
Dyssodia tenuiloba	Dahlberg daisy
Gaillardia grandiflora	Blanket flower or gaillardia 'Red Plume' (AAS), 'Yellow Sun'
Gomphrena globosa	Globe amaranth or gomphrena 'Lavender Lady', 'Bicolor Rose', and the 'Woodcreek' color series
Heliotropium arborescens	Heliotrope or cherry-pie plant 'Mini-Marine' and 'Blue Wonder'
*Melampodium paludosum**	Melampodium or butter daisy 'Million Gold', 'Medallion', 'Derby'
Petunia hybrids	Petunia 'Wave' color series 'Cascadia' color series
Salvia coccinea	Salvia 'Lady in Red' and 'Starry-eyed Mixed Colors'

Salvia farinacea	Blue salvia 'Victoria' and 'Strata' (AAS)
Sanvitalia procumbens	Creeping zinnia 'Mandarin Orange' (AAS)
Tithonia rotundifolia	Mexican sunflower 'Torch', 'Goldfinger', and 'Sundance'
Verbena × *speciosa*	Verbena 'Imagination', 'Pretty' color series, 'Tropicana' color series, 'Parasol' (AAS), and 'Hot Streak Salmon'
Zinnia angustifolia	Zinnia 'Crystal White' (AAS), 'Tropical Snow', 'Classic', and 'White Star'

*Over the years, melampodium has never performed poorly in our trials. No matter our growing conditions, it always ranks as a top performer. The two-foot-high 'Million Gold' was a showstopper all season. 'Derby' has a shorter plant.

PERENNIALS (winter hardy here)

Coreopsis verticillata	Coreopsis, threadleaf 'Moonbeam' and 'Zagreb'
Euphorbia myrsinites	Myrtle euphorbia (grown for its gray-green foliage)
Heuchera sp.	American alumroot or heuchera 'Eco Magnififolia', 'Ruby Veil', 'Chocolate Ruffles'
Hibiscus moscheutos	Rose mallow or swamp rose, series of colors
Leucanthemum × *superbum*	Shasta daisy 'Becky'
Lobelia speciosa (hybrids, using germplasm from *L. cardinalis* in the crosses)	Cardinal flower hybrids 'Compliment Scarlet', 'Compliment Blue', 'Pink Flamingo'
Nepeta faassenii	Catmint, dwarf 'Blue Carpet'
Perovskia atriplicifolia	Russian sage

Rudbeckia fulgida var. *sullivanti*	Black-eyed Susan 'Goldsturm'
Salvia guaranitica	Salvia, anise-scented 'Brazilian Blue'
Salvia × *superba* (sterile hybrid)	Salvia, blue perennial 'Blue Queen', 'May Night'
Sedum spectabile	Sedum, autumn, or showy stonecrop 'Brilliant' and 'Indian Chief'
Solidago rugosa	Goldenrod, rough-leafed 'Crown of Rays'
Stachys sp.	Lamb's ear, 'Big Ears' (originally known as 'Countess Helene Von Stein')
Tanacetum parthenium	Feverfew, double-flowered 'Ultra Double'
Verbena bonariensis	Verbena, Argentine
Verbena canadensis and hybrids	Verbena, perennial 'Homestead Purple' 'Graystone Daphne' light pink 'Fiesta' bright pink 'Marie's Rose' reddish purple 'Pink Sunrise' coral pink 'Snowflurry' white 'Summer Blaze' clear red
Veronica × *hybrida*	Speedwell, spike speedwell 'Sunny Border Blue'

HERBS

Cymbopogon nardus	Citronella grass (grown as an annual)
Cynara cardunculus	Cardoon or cardoni (biennial)
Foeniculum vulgare	Fennel, bronze 'Purpurascens' (perennial)
Monarda citriodora	Lemon bergamot 'Lambada' (annual)
Ocimum spp.	Basil (annual)
Ocimum sanctum	'Purple Holy Basil'
O. basilicum	'Purple Osmin'
O. basilicum	'Red Rubin'

O. basilicum	'African Blue'
O. basilicum	'Siam Queen' (AAS) (Thai basil)
Origanum sp.	Ornamental oregano 'Herrenhausen' (perennial), 'Aureum' (golden creeping oregano, perennial)
Pelargonium sp.	Scented geranium, variegated, orange-scented 'Snowflake' (not frost hardy)
Spilanthes oleracea	Toothache plant (grow as an annual) (pale yellow, gumdroplike flowers)

In addition to the field trials, **hanging basket trials** were conducted by Terri Woods Starman, Ph.D., and Millie S. Williams to find alternatives to the kinds that are typically planted by greenhouses. Of the fifty kinds of plants studied, these were the best all-around performers. Of these, only the verbena is hardy enough to transplant to the garden in the fall for re-use the following year.

FLOWERS FOR HANGING BASKETS

Abutilon × *hybridum*	Flowering maple 'Apricot' (outstanding hummingbird flower)
Cuphea hyssopifolia	Mexican heather 'Dynamite'
Evolvulus nuttallianus	Evolvulus glomeratus 'Blue Daze'
Scaevola aemula	Fan flower 'New Wonder'
Tibouchina urvilleana	Glory bush or princess flower 'Spanish Shawl' (purplish bronze foliage, pink flowers)
Helichrysum sp.	Helichrysum 'Golden Beauty'
Portulaca sp.	Purslane 'Apricot'
Pentas lanceolata	Star clusterflower 'Starburst' (compact grower)
Streptocarpus saxorum (formerly *Streptocarpella saxorum*)	Streptocarpella or Cape Primrose
Verbena sp.	Verbena 'Trailing Katie'

ORNAMENTAL GRASSES

Pennisetum alopecuroides   Dwarf fountain grass 'Hameln'
   'Hameln'

University of Georgia

The University of Georgia's flower trials on their campus at Athens, Georgia, are among the best-run in the South. Ms. Meg Green, trialmaster, sent the following report to *GrowerTalks* magazine. The report is reprinted by permission.

Ms. Green commented, "The test year was very hot and very dry. My personal picks from our annual trials were *Scaevola* 'Outback Purple Fan', *Zinnia* 'Profusion Cherry' (AAS), and Cascading fuchsia. However, the favorites of people attending the trial were blue angelonia and an ornamental *Pennisetum* (fountain grass)."

The best new varieties in our trials were

> *Torenia* 'Summer Wave', rated excellent
>
> *Brachycome* or Swan River daisy 'Outback'
>
> *Plectranthus* 'Athens Gem'
>
> *Duranta* 'Southern blue', a woody shrub, grown here as an annual

The top performers, new or established varieties, were

> *Celosia* 'New Look'
>
> *Impatiens* 'Carnival Orange'
>
> *Petunia* 'Fantasy Carmine', 'Misty Lilac Wave', 'Surfinia Mini Brilliant Pink'
>
> *Portulaca* 'Yubi' color series
>
> *Salvia* 'Red Hot Sally'
>
> *Scaevola* 'Outback Purple Fan'
>
> *Periwinkle* 'Pacifica White'
>
> *Zinnia* 'Profusion Cherry' (All-America Selections Winner)

Oklahoma State University Trials At Their Oklahoma City Campus

Oklahoma City can be hot and very dry. Here's how Haldor Howard, trial manager at the Oklahoma State University flower trials at the Oklahoma City campus, described the growing season for the test year: "Heat came in early, stayed, and was made worse by a prolonged drought."

Mr. Haldor's report appeared in *GrowerTalks* magazine and is reprinted by permission. His trials were sizable and included a few varieties not reported by other trial managers. His personal picks were 'Strata', a silver-and-blue variety from *Salvia farinacea*, and 'Yubi Rose', from *Portulaca*. But the favorites of home gardeners visiting the trials were an unnamed purple-foliage ornamental okra, and a purple pearl millet with a large, cattaillike flower and seed head.

The top performers in the trial were

Celosia 'New Look' and 'Prestige Scarlet'

Dianthus 'Diamond Purple' and 'Diamond Carmine Rose'

Impatiens 'Showstopper Tropical Punch'

Melampodium paludosum 'Derby' and 'Showstar'

Portulaca 'Yubi' color series: 'Pink', 'Rose', 'Scarlet', 'Red', 'Light Pink', and 'White'

Salvia farinacea 'Strata' (All-America Selections award winner)

Salvia splendens 'Vista Red' and 'Vista Lavender'

Verbena 'Tapien Pink' and 'Temari Violet'

Vinca or periwinkle 'Heatwave'

Sterling Garden Center

Long summers, quite hot, often humid . . . that sums up the growing season in Columbia, South Carolina. The predominant soil type is sand, but all the soils around Columbia need frequent fortification with organic matter to help them store water and plant nutrients. In the mid 1990s, Sterling Garden Center set up business near the downtown area of Columbia and has established a reputation for supplying well-grown plants of southeastern natives and the latest in adapted cultivars. Fran and Walter Bull, whom I met when we featured their home landscape on *The Victory Garden*, supplied this list of summer and fall flowers, all notably resistant to zone 8 heat and humidity.

Autumn sage (*Salvia greggii*). Comes in several blossom colors. Bloom is intermittent from spring through fall, and its bushes are generally evergreen. Over the years they become woody and need thinning and pruning. It is a good hummingbird flower.

Belize sage (*Salvia miniata*). This sage is notable for its glossy, dark green foliage and very dark red blossoms. It blooms from midsummer on. (Author's note: I tried Belize sage in my zone 7 garden and it winter-killed. But, boy! was it a gorgeous plant all summer long. It was a magnet for hummingbirds.)

Bloodflower (*Asclepias curassavica*). Red and orange bicolored blossoms on three-foot-high plants. For us, it blooms within ninety days of seeding in ground beds. It is a choice host plant for monarch butterflies.

Cassias (*Cassia* sp.). All the cassias flourish in our summer heat and humidity, but only a few species will survive our winters and grow into shrubs. *C. corymbosa* var. *bicapsularis* makes an airy, yellow-flowered woody plant here. All the visitors from up North want to know its name.

Cosmos (*Cosmos bipinnatus* and *C. sulphureus*). We sell plants of the pink, purple and white *C. bipinnatus* and the yellow, gold, and deep orange *C. sulphureus*. Many of our sales are for late summer planting to produce fall color. Gardeners see the plantings of cosmos in the medians on nearby interstate freeways and are inspired to try them. Of the two, *C. sulphureus* is the more heat resistant. Both species produce lots of seeds that are relished by finches.

Mexican bush sage (*Salvia leucantha*). Fran says, "This has long been a personal favorite. The long, lavender or purple spikes come in late summer when garden color is otherwise scarce. It is perfectly hardy here and will bloom the first summer after being set out in the spring."

Pentas (*Pentas lanceolata*). The various colors of pentas are gaining in popularity in the Columbia area, as gardeners learn how well it performs in our heat, and see how butterflies are drawn to it. We sell both the dwarf and tall types to grow as annuals.

Petunia integrifolia. This small-flowered, spreading petunia has no common name. It is a different species from the multiflora and grandiflora garden hybrids. Our *P. integrifolia* plants bloomed all last summer, survived the winter, and are again covered with multitudes of blossoms. The choice in colors is limited at present.

Petunia. 'Wave' color series 'Purple Wave' puts on an unbelievable show of color all summer long on low, spreading plants. It needs more plant food than standard garden petunias to maintain its vigor. We sell it for use as a summer groundcover and to trail over the edges of planter boxes, large containers, and hanging baskets.

Pincushion flower (*Scabiosa columbaria*, formerly *S. caucasica*) 'Butterfly Blue'. This is an amazing plant. It blooms intermittently through mild winters here and shows color every month of the year. Yet, it endures our summers despite its rather small frame. The blossoms last well when cut.

Pineapple sage (*Salvia elegans*). The attractive, velvety summer foliage on tall plants is as strong an attraction as the spikes of red blossoms that come in late summer and continue through fall. All parts of the plant are pleasantly fragrant, and are used in teas and potpourris.

Sapphire sage (*Salvia guaranitica*). Before we learned about this appealing common name, we labeled our plants by the botanical name, and it has stuck. This deep violet-blue salvia is a favorite of our staff because it is virtually trouble free and blooms for months on end. The plants grow to three to four feet in height and gradually widen into sizable clumps. It forms sparse spikes of tubular blossoms about 1½ inches long. The way hummingbirds come to it, you would think it was a blazing red instead of blue.

Strawflower (*Helichrysum bracteatum*). Ordinarily this everlasting flower blooms right through our summers, but an exceptionally wet and hot summer can wipe it out. During dry summers each plant forms dozens of blossoms with satin-shiny petals that can be cut at the immature stage for drying. You can buy standard varieties that grow to a height of two to three feet, or the dwarf 'Bright Bikini' (mixed colors) that seldom tops one foot in height.

Swamp sunflower (*Helianthus angustifolius*). Long-lived, rugged and showy, swamp sunflower forms spreading clumps that have to be thinned and reduced to keep it in check. On dry soil it will reach five feet in height, but on moist soil it may top eight feet. Trimming or pinching back the stems in midsummer can keep down the height considerably. It begins blooming in early October and stays in color through fall frost.

Geo. W. Park Seed Co.

I am fortunate to have known the Park family, owners of Park Seed Co., Greenwood, South Carolina, for about forty years. One of the younger generation, Karen Park Jennings, Senior Vice President of the company, sent me the following list of heat- and humidity-resistant ornamentals. All of them have performed well in the Park Seed Co. trials, either in containers or ground beds.

Botanical Name	Common Name
Brugsmansia cultivars	Angel's trumpet
Coleus cultivar	Coleus 'Trailing Red' (sun tolerant)
Fuchsia cultivars	Fuchsia 'Chimes', 'Swing', and 'Florabelle' bloom until very hot weather arrives
Gazania rigens (Must have perfect drainage)	Gazania 'Daybreak'
Impatiens walleriana	Impatiens 'Victorian Rose'
Ipomoea batatas	Ornamental sweet potato 'Margarita'
Lantana cultivar	Lantana 'Tangerine'
Mandevilla splendens	Mandevilla 'Janelle' and 'Leah'
Musa zebrina	Ornamental banana
Salix integra	Willow 'Hakuro Nishiki'
Scaevola aemula	Fan flower, blue
Strobilanthes dyeranus	Persian shield

Callaway Gardens, Pine Mountain, Georgia

I drove the four hours to Callaway Gardens several times a year to meet the production crew from WGBH-TV, Boston. We would labor from four to eight hours, taping shows for *The Victory Garden.* At the time, Callaway Gardens employed Lucinda Mays as a horticulturist, and later promoted her to Curator of Horticulture. Lucinda appeared as a guest on the shows a few times, then became the southern host of what we called *Victory Garden South.* I moved on to do shows further afield. Lucinda excelled in designing gardens and tried many flowers that were new to the area. She did a great job for Callaway Gardens and became a popular personage among the viewers of PBS shows.

In the late '90s, Lucinda retired from Callaway, returned to her native Nebraska, and started a family. Before she left horticulture for parenting, she gave me a list of heat- and humidity-resistant flowers that had performed well in her zone 7b garden at Pine Mountain, Georgia.

Artemisia or wormwood. The silvery white 'Powis Castle' is especially good, and grows rather slowly, unlike some other wormwoods that flower and have to be cut back in late June.

Balloon vine or love-in-a-puff (*Cardiospermum halicacabum*). This is a novel annual that elicits many questions. It climbs to eight or ten feet and has small, white flowers, but the inflated pods are the attraction. They are about one inch in diameter, faintly three-lobed, and somewhat furry to the touch. The foliage is naturally pale green. We grow it from seeds.

Banana, ornamental (*Musa* sp.). We grow the red dwarf ornamental banana in corners protected from the wind, for its long, broad, dark, reddish-brown foliage. It is not winter-hardy for us.

Blanket flower (*Gaillardia pulchella*). A brilliant annual with daisylike red, yellow, and orange blossoms. It will come back from dropped seeds for several years.

China rose (*Rosa chinensis* 'Mutabilis'). Large, disease-resistant bush, winter-hardy here. Its loosely-double blooms open yellow and age to pink and crimson to give a multicolored effect.

Coleus, sun tolerant (*Solenostemon* 'Volcano'). This grows into a large-leafed subshrub for us. We propagate it from cuttings.

Copper plant or copper leaf (*Acalypha wilkesiana*). Shrubby plants, with large, shiny, brightly marked leaves. Not winter-hardy for us.

Coral bells (*Heuchera sp.*) 'Palace Purple'. Colors up best with afternoon shade under our intense summer sun.

Cosmos sulphureus varieties, especially 'Bright Lights' and 'Lemon Twist'. These are so brilliant that we use them to light up beds along the walks leading to Victory Garden South. They attract butterflies and seed-eating finches.

English ivy (*Hedera helix* 'Gold Child'). We find many uses for this green-and-gold variegated ivy, as it thrives in full sun without burning around the margins or fading. We propagate it vegetatively.

Euphorbia cotinifolia. A superior ornamental, perhaps held back for its lack of a common name. Bronzy red foliage all summer long is its main appeal.

Fennel, bronze (*Foeniculum vulgare*). Tall, erect plants, with ferny, bronze, anise-scented foliage. We grow this biennial from seeds.

Hibiscus 'Red Shield'. We were one of the first gardens in these parts to plant this dark purple subshrub, grown for its foliage. It grows to a height of six or eight feet in a single season. We use it for backgrounds in borders, where it sets off the bright colors of fall flowers. You may have to search for a source.

Impatiens, New Guinea (*I. hawkerii*). We like 'Tango'. It makes rather large, bushy plants with dark bronzy foliage and brilliant orange flowers. Needs afternoon shade, good drainage, and ample water.

Jerusalem sage (*Phlomis fruticosa*). Has gray foliage and yellow, clawlike blossoms in whorls around its stems. It grows to a height of two and one-half to three feet.

Lantana. We grow both the trailing and shrubby forms. Lantana has to be cut back and mulched here to overwinter reliably. It is a favorite of butterflies. We wear gloves when handling the plants or weeding among them, as it can cause contact dermatitis.

Lemon bergamot (*Monarda citriodora*). Confusingly referred to also as "lemon mint." A native annual, it draws hummingbirds, butterflies, and seed-eating finches. It completes its life cycle in July and dries up, but volunteer seedlings come up to give a second flush of lavender color through the fall months. The plants are erect and two to two and one-half feet tall.

Mandevilla. The bushy form that is called "Dipladenia" here is usually grown in containers and trained to a shrub form. It produces loads of tubular, pink flowers. We also grow many plants of the vining mandevilla, and have for several years. It is one of our most heat-resistant annual flowering vines. We bring the containers indoors for the winter.

Melampodium (*M. paludosum*). We grow this yellow, daisy-flowered plant as annual. No "wimp," this one; it keeps on flowering through the hottest days.

Mexican bush salvia (*Salvia leucantha*). One of the best shrub-like perennials, with gray foliage and long purple spikes. It flowers late in the summer but is attractive all season.

Mondo grass (*Ophiopogon planiscapus*). Very dark purple, grasslike plants with pink flowers and blue-green berries. Winter-hardy here. We use it in containers and for edgings.

Peppers, ornamental (*Capsicum frutescens*). We grow several varieties, and are particularly fond of the tall 'Tabasco' with its upstanding yellow fruit that turns bright red late in the season.

Petunia, perennial (*Petunia integrifolia*). We grow the magenta-flowered variety. It has medium-sized flowers on spreading plants. It overwinters in our hardiness zone 7b.

Plumbago (*P. capensis*). We depend on plumbago for light blue accent plants that stay in color all summer. Only rarely will it survive winters here.

Purple heart (*Secreasea pallida 'Purpurea'*). Sprawling plants to sixteen inches in height, with intensely violet-purple, canoe-like leaves. We grow it as an annual.

Russian sage (*Perovskia atriplicifolia*). Wonderful, lacy, silvery-blue, see-through plants with dainty lavender flower spikes, two and one-half to three feet tall.

Salvia 'East Friesland'. Its purple flowers drop after a few weeks, leaving attractive spikes of showy, bronze-purple bracts that resemble blossoms.

Salvias from Mexico and Central America such as *S. guaranitica* and other perennial salvias from these subtropical habitats do better in afternoon shade here.

Scaevola (*S. aemula*). This is a relatively new plant for us. We grow it mostly in hanging baskets with afternoon shade. Its short branches with lavender-blue, fanlike flowers trail nicely.

Star cluster flower or Egyptian star cluster flower (*Pentas lanceolata*). A very durable summer flower, attractive to butterflies. We plant several colors of it, but are partial to the dark red and pink shades.

Silver dollar tree (*Eucalyptus cinerea*). We grow it to use as foliage in arrangements. It is a gangly, fast-growing tree with round, blue-gray leaves used fresh or dried. It often freezes to the ground and occasionally winter-kills.

Silver lace vine (*Fallopia baldschuanica*, syn. *Polygonum auberti*). This strong perennial vine tends to take over large areas, so we have to trim it back to keep it in bounds. It blooms with numerous racemes of fragrant white flowers in May, then reblooms in September. We got our original start from seeds.

Sweet potato, ornamental (*Ipomoea batatas* 'Blackie'). We use it as a trailing plant in containers and hanging baskets, and for foliage accents in borders. It has very dark purple, deeply cut leaves and short runners.

Tropical or Texas salvia (*Salvia coccinea*). Both 'Lady in Red' and 'Cherry Blossom' grow well for us and reseed generously. Both draw hummingbirds and butterflies.

White gaura (*Gaura lindheimeri*). The thirty-inch perennial native wildflower is long-lived here.

Wishbone flower or bluewings (*Torenia fournieri* 'Clown'). We grow the pink, white, blue, or purple colors in the 'Clown' series from seeds. The plants bloom all summer in full sun, but probably could benefit from afternoon shade further south.

Zinnia, giant, or large-flowered (*Z. elegans*). We have found 'Scarlet Splendor' and 'Zenith Yellow' to be fairly resistant to mildew and other foliage diseases here. We grow this annual from seeds. The plants grow to about two and one-half feet at maturity and the blossoms may reach four to five inches in diameter.

Zinnia angustifolia, including dwarf selections from the golden wild species, and the cultivar 'Star White' tolerate extreme dryness here and keep on blooming.

Lucinda went on to say, "Some flowers seem to melt out when we have prolonged rains during the summer. Both strawflower (*Helichrysum bracteatum*) and *Verbena tenuisecta* can rot if we experience back-to-back summer rains during hot, humid weather. False licorice (*Helichrysum petiolare*) and blanket flower (*Gaillardia pulchella*) can also suffer the same fate. Unfortunately, so do the new generation of petunias, including 'Purple Wave' and the Supertunias.

"We have so many visitors to Callaway Gardens that we try to have lots of color to greet them, spring, summer, and fall. Flowers that can be planted in late spring for summerlong bloom are very valuable to us. We continue to evaluate new cultivars from seed companies and nurseries, particularly those down in Florida, for resistance to heat and humidity."

Dell Ratcliffe, Editor, *Country Shepherd Herb News*

Dell, her family, and friends publish this newsletter from Comer, Georgia, a little town near the Savannah River in hardiness zone 7a. She responded to my inquiry about bulletproof flowers with some (forgive the pun) sage advice to southern gardeners.

"I like plants that I can just set out and not worry about for the next several months," Dell said, "but the problem that goes with that situation is how to handle spacing of plants. If you leave room for the plant to grow to mature size, you will have too much soil exposed between plants early on, and weeds will spring up. I prefer to mulch the bare soil between widely spaced plants. The mulch smothers most of the weeds, and those that do come up are easy to pull out.

"We grow flowers as well as herbs in our garden, but not all herbs will survive our summer heat and humidity and still look good until fall. Here are the really rugged survivors."

HERBS

Anise-scented marigold or Mexican tarragon (*Tagetes lucida*). This one stays dark green all summer, and sets on hundreds of small yellow flowers two or three weeks before the first fall frost. Visitors to our farm love its strong, sweet, anise fragrance. The plants survive most winters here. We divide the crowns every third year.

Basil (*Ocimum basilicum*). 'African Blue' and 'Sweet Aussie' look good all summer here, as does a tall one we call "tree basil." We try to keep the seed spikes trimmed off.

Cardamon (*Elettaria cardamomum*). Another pretty, yet durable, tropical-looking herb. We have to overwinter it indoors.

Garlic chives (*Allium tuberosum*). If we don't allow the clumps to dry out during droughts, they look good all summer. The clusters of white, starlike flowers on eighteen-inch stems are quite pretty in July and August, and are good to pull apart and eat in salads.

Lavender (*Lavandula* sp.). The cultivars in the English lavender group will survive for years here, given good drainage and plenty of dolomitic limestone. Most of the other lavender species have to be treated as annuals, but some of the Lavandin hybrids* have proven hardy. What seems to kill lavender and rosemary here is winter weather that changes from mild to quite cold so rapidly that the evergreen plants have no opportunity to harden off.

Lemon grass (*Cymbopogon citratus*). We grow this one as an ornamental. Heat doesn't faze it, but it must have plenty of water. I have to take divisions indoors in the fall to overwinter plants to start my next year's garden. Vetiver (*Vetiveria zizanioides*), another grasslike herb, has to be treated in the same way.

Lemon verbena (*Aloysia triphylla*). Grows into a large bush here and is virtually problem-free. It makes a billowy shrub with light green foliage and fluffy panicles of white flowers during July and August. It will survive mild winters outdoors here if mulched with pinestraw.

Perilla (*Perilla frutescens*). Folks often confuse the purple beefsteak plant with the dark-purple basils, but of the two, perilla can stand up better to hot, humid weather. It does have a problem; it drops seeds which come up all over the garden.

Rosemary (*Rosmarinus officinalis*). Providing we give our plants near-perfect drainage and plenty of lime, rosemary will survive our winters and grow to considerable size. Irrigating rosemary heavily after a long, dry spell can be fatal to the plants.

Salvias, edible. Of these, pineapple sage and honeydew melon sage hold up best during hot, humid weather. Plants of garden sage often die in midsummer because of root rot or nematode damage.

Salvias, ornamental. We grow several kinds in our landscape for dependable all-summer color. Most will not overwinter here, but Mexican bush salvia is an exception. It will survive all but the coldest winters.

Scented geraniums (*Pelargonium* sp.). The big, robust cultivars stand up best to our summers, especially the old-fashioned, rose-scented and rose-cinnamon selections.

*"Lavandin" is the name given to lavenders hybridized by or for the perfume industry for intense fragrance. Some of the many named lavandins are hardy in zone 7, notably 'Provence'.

OTHER ORNAMENTALS

Ginger lilies (*Hedychium coronarium*). We grow the white one. It blooms in July but looks good all season. The plants grow four or five feet tall and the flowers are intensely fragrant. The rhizomes survive the winters here without mulching.

Lion's ear or lion's tail (*Leonotis leonurus*). Most folks around here don't know this plant, but they admire it when it is in flower. It is a pretty thing, with gray foliage and furry, orange-yellow flowers on erect plants, about three feet tall.

Ornamental peppers. 'Thai Hot', with its tiny, slender fruit, 'Tabasco', and 'Jalapeno' do especially well here. We recommend them for bright color among herb plants, which otherwise have to depend on rather subtle shades of gray, green, and silver for landscape effect.

Tallahassee Nurseries

Twice during recent years I have lectured at Tallahassee Nurseries. Located in Florida's capital city, in hardiness zone 8b, it is a big, full-service garden center and landscape nursery. Area master gardeners maintain an evaluation garden on the nursery grounds, where new cultivars are tried. Sue Watkins, a staff horticulturist, sent me this list of ornamentals that have established a good record for surviving their long, hot, humid summers. The notes and descriptions are hers. Truthfully, I have never seen some of these, but if they are on this list, they have been grown successfully for some time in the Tallahassee area.

Artemisia 'Valerie Finnis" and 'Silver King'. Other varieties melt out with summer fungus diseases. All grow better here during the winter.

Balloon flower (*Platycodon* sp.)

Begonias, wax-leaved (*Begonia semperflorens* × cultorum hybrids). We grow them with morning sun or in moderate shade.*

Black-eyed Susan (*Rudbeckia fulgida* var. *sullivantii* 'Goldsturm' and 'Herbstonne')

Bloodflower or **milkweed** (*Asclepias curassavica*)

Blue daze (*Evolvulus glomerata* 'Blue Daze')*

California bush daisy (*Euryops pectinata*)

Canna, several named cultivars

Cat's whiskers (*Orthosiphon stamineus*)

Celosia 'New Look' and *C. plumosa* 'Flaming Feather'*

Clerodendrum. Several species and selections grow well here: bleeding heart vine (*C. thompsoniae*), butterfly vine (*C. ugandense*), and harlequin glory (*C. trichotomum*). Avoid *C. bungei;* it can become a nuisance.

Coleus. Sue says, "The new 'Sunlover' series is fantastic!"*

Cleome or **spiderflower** (*Cleome hassleriana*)*

Coreopsis, threadleaf (*C. verticillata* 'Moonbeam' and 'Zagreb')

Cosmos sulphureus varieties*

Creeping Charlie, creeping Jenny or **moneywort** (*Lysimachia nummularia* 'Eco Dark Satin')

Cuphea. Several species grow well here: *C. micropetala*, Mexican heather (*C. hyssopifolia*), *C. llavea*, and cigar plant (*C. ignea*)

Cupflower (*Nierembergia hippomanica* 'Mont Blanc')*

Dahlberg daisy (*Dyssodia tenuiloba*)*

Dianthus. The best show of color from the annual varieties comes in the spring, but they also look good during the summer.

Fan flower (*Scaevola aemula*)

Firespike or **cardinal's guard** (*Odontonema strictum*)

Fleabane (*Erigeron karvinskianus* 'Profusion')

Globe amaranth (*Gomphrena globosa*)*

Glory bush (*Tibouchina urvilleana*)

Hawaiian snowbush (*Breynia nivosa*). White, green, and pink variegated foliage.

Hibiscus, both the tropical hybrids and the native mallows. The tropicals have to be taken indoors for the winter.

Impatiens or **busy Lizzie** (*I. walleriana* varieties). Need moderate shade here.

Japanese aster (*Gymnaster savatieri*)

Jerusalem sage (*Phlomis fruticosa*)

Jewels of Opar (*Talinum paniculatum*). Sue says it is very invasive.

Justicia carnea. Has many common names: Brazilian plume, plume flower, flamingo plant, paradise plant, king's crown, etc., etc. Partial to deep shade or morning sun and afternoon shade.

Lantana. Cultivars are very heat resistant here and attract butterflies.

Madagascar periwinkle (*Catharanthus roseus*).* It may reseed but the volunteers won't come true to type.

Mandevilla cultivars such as 'Alice du Pont' (*Mandevilla* × *amabilis*)

Melampodium (*M. paludosum*)*

Mexican bush sage (*Salvia leucantha*). Needs partial shade here.

Mexican sunflower (*Tithonia rotundifolia*)*

Obedient plant (*Physostegia virginiana*). Needs partial shade here.

Peacock ginger. Several species of the genus *Kaempferia* do well here in light to moderate shade.

Peppers, ornamental (*Capsicum annuum* and *C. frutescens*)*

Phlox, summer (*P. paniculata* cultivars). They appreciate shade during August.

Plumbago or **cape plumbago** (*P. capensis*)

Polka dot plant (*Hypoestes phyllostachya*). Will tolerate sun or light to moderate shade and will survive mild winters here.

Portulaca or **rose moss** (*P. grandiflora*). We like the varieties that stay open longer.*

Purple prairie coneflower (*Echinacea purpurea*). Several varieties do well here.

Porterweed (*Stachytarpheta jamaicensis*). We grow it as an annual here.

Purple heart or **purple creeper** (*Setcreasea pallida* 'Purpurea')

Purslane (*Portulaca oleracea*). The flowering varieties (not the garden weed) are treated as annuals here.

Ruellia (*Ruellia brittoniana*). The cultivar 'Chi Chi' is sometimes called 'hardy pink petunia,' despite there being no botanical relationship between *Ruellia* and *Petunia*.

Russian sage (*Perovskia atriplicifolia*)

Salvia coccinea. Varieties such as 'Lady in Red', 'Coral Nymph', and 'White Dove' tolerate shade and come back from volunteer seedlings.*

Salvias. Those from Mexico and Central America, such as *S. guaranitica*, do best here in partial shade. Some of the *Salvia superba* cultivars don't show much stamina in Tallahassee summers.

Shrimp plant (*Justicia brandegeana* cultivars)

Skullcap (*Scutellaria* 'Purple Fountain')

Star clusterflower (*Pentas lanceolata*)*

Strawflower or everlasting (*Helichrysum bracteatum*)*

Verbena canadensis and ***V. tenuisecta*** hybrids and selections

White gaura (*Gaura lindheimeri*)

Wishbone flower (*Torenia fournieri*)*

Veronica cultivars such as 'Goodness Grows' and 'Blue Charm'

Zinnias, especially the narrow-leaved *Z. angustifolia* varieties*

*These plants act as annuals in Tallahassee.

The Daniel Stowe Botanical Garden

One of the most exciting botanical gardens in the Southeast is a new kid on the block: the Daniel Stowe Botanical Garden in Belmont, North Carolina, near Gastonia. Its aptly named director, Mike Bush, supplied climatalogical data for their hottest year to date, during which the flowers he listed were grown. Look at Mike's figures for heat and rainfall.

"Between June 17 and September 5, we endured fifty-six days of 90-degree-plus weather, which included four hot spells:

The longest stretch was July 2–22, twenty-one days;
Next longest stretch was June 17–26, ten days;
Third was August 27–September 3, eight days;
and fourth was August 10–15, six days.

"The remaining hot days were scattered through the balance of summer, and weather ranged from wet to dry; here's the pattern of summer rainfall:

Mid June to the end of June, 2.47 inches;
Month of July, 6.85 inches;
Month of August, .24 inches.

Herbaceous Perennials	Generally Accepted Common Name, if Different
Artemisia 'Powis Castle', 'Valerie Finnis'	
Coreopsis 'Zagreb'	
Dahlia 'Bronze Bishop'	
Hemerocallis 'Happy Returns'	Daylily
Hibiscus coccineus (red), and 'Blue River II'	Native hardy hibiscus
Hibiscus 'Red Shield'	
Hylotelephium 'Vera Jameson'	The new name for *Sedum*
Phlox paniculata 'Sandra' *	Summer or perennial phlox
Salvia uliginosa	Bog sage
Salvia guaranitica	Brazilian sage
S. guaranitica 'Argentine Skies'	
S. greggii 'Marischino'	Texas or autumn sage
Setcreasea 'Purple Heart'	Purple creeper
Spirea 'Goldmound'	
Spirea 'Lime Mound'	
Stachys 'Big Ears'	Giant lamb's ears
Stokesia 'Klaus Jelitto'	
Verbena 'Homestead Purple'	
Verbena red form	
Veronica 'Goodness Grows'	Speedwell

Subshrubs

Clerodendrum ugandense

Lantana 'Miss Huff'

Annuals

Coleus spp.	
Emilia javanica	Tassel flower
Euphorbia marginata 'Summer Icicle'*	Snow on the Mountain
Evolvulus 'Blue Daze'	German violet
Exacum affine 'Midget Blue'	
Gomphrena haageana 'Strawberry Fields' 'Purple Gnome'	Bachelor button
Impatiens spp.	
Melampodium paludosum	Butter daisy
Monarda citriodora	Lemon bergamot
Pentas spp.	Star clusterflower
Petunia integrifolia	No common name
Phlox drummondi 'Phlox of Sheep'+	Annual phlox
Ricinus communis 'Impala'	Castor bean
Salvia coccinea 'Coral Nymph'/ 'Cherry Blossom'	Bicolor Texas salvia (They look identical to us.)
Salvia coccinea 'Lady in Red'	Texas salvia
S. farinacea 'Victory White', 'Victory Blue'	Mealycup salvia
Sanvitalia procumbens	Creeping zinnia
Scaevola aemula 'New Wonder'	Fanflower
Tagetes patula 'Tiger Eyes'	French marigold
Verbena 'Imagination'	
Zinnia angustifolia 'Tropic Snow'	Narrow-leafed zinnia
Z. elegans 'Double Envy'	Giant green zinnia

Vines

Lonicera sempervirens 'John Chapman'	Native honeysuckle
Thunbergia alata	Clock vine

*Performed especially well.
+Rebloomed profusely three weeks after being cut back.

Appendix

Here are the addresses for organizations, products, and services mentioned in the text.

Organizations and Their Publications

American Horticultural Society. Phone them at (800) 777-7931, ext. 45.

AHS Plant Heat-Zone Map. Phone the American Horticultural Society to order.

USDA Hardiness Zone Map. This large and beautiful two-foot by three-foot poster map can be ordered by phoning the Agricultural Research Service, USDA.

Catalogs or Price Lists

Caladium World, P.O. Box 629, Sebring, FL 33871-0629 (orders for 25 or more corms)

Forest Farm, 990 Tetherow Road, Williams, OR 97544-9599

Goldsmith Seeds, Inc., Box 1349, Gilroy, CA 95201

Old House Gardens, 536 Third Street, Ann Arbor, MI 48103-4957 (heirloom bulbs)

Park Seed Company, 1 Parkton Ave., Greenwood, SC 29647-0001 (flower seeds and plants)

Plant Delights Nursery, 1941 Sauls Road, Raleigh, NC 27603 (plants)

Stokes Seeds, P.O. Box 548, Buffalo, NY 14240 (specializes in ornamental bananas, flowering gingers, and tropical foliage plants)

Stokes Tropicals, P.O. Box 9868, New Iberia, LA 70562

Southern Perennials and Herbs, 98 Bridges Road, Tylertown, MS 39677-9338. E-mail: sph@neosoft.com

Territorial Seed Company, P.O. Box 157, Cottage Grove, OR 97424-0061

The Great Plant Company, P.O. Box 1041, New Hartford, CT 06057

Thompson & Morgan, P.O. Box 1308, Jackson NJ 08527-0308

Wayside Gardens, P.O. Box 1, Hodges, SC 29695-0001

Woodlanders, Inc., 1128 Colleton Ave., Aiken, SC 29801

Authors and Their Horticultural Reference Books and CDs

Ajilvsgi, Geyata, *Wildflowers of Texas*. Bryan, Texas: Shearer Publishing.

Armitrage, Allan, Ph.D. *The Educated Gardener, Vol. 1, Herbaceous Perennial Plants*. CD distributed by PlantAmerica. E-mail: support@plantamerica.com.

Barton, Barbara, *Gardening by Mail*. Boston, Mass.: Mariner Books, Houghton Mifflin Co.

Bender, Steve, Editor, *The Southern Living Garden Book*, Birmingham, Alabama: Oxmoor House. (out of print)

Booth, Charles O., *An Encyclopedia of Annual and Biennial Garden Plants*. London: Faber and Faber Ltd.

Bryan, John, *Bulbs*, two-volume set. Portland, Oregon: Timber Press.

Chaplin, Lois Trigg, *The Southern Gardener's Book of Lists*. Dallas, Texas: Taylor Publishing Co.

Dirr, Michael A., Ph.D., *Manual of Woody Landscape Plants, Their Identification, Ornamental Characteristics, Culture, Propagation and Uses*. Portland, Oregon: Stipes Publishing. (a college textbook, also suitable for avid home gardeners)

Dirr, Michael A., Ph.D., *Photo Library of Woody Landscape Plants*. Portland, Oregon: Timber Press and Stipes Publishing. Contact www.plantamerica.com.

Griffiths, Mark, *The New Royal Horticultural Society Dictionary: Index of Garden Plants*. Portland, Oregon: Timber Press.

Lawrence, Elizabeth, *A Southern Garden: A Handbook for the Middle South* (reprint). Chapel Hill, N.C.: University of North Carolina Press.

Lawton, Barbara Perry, *Magic of Irises*. Golden, Colorado: Fulcrum Publishing.

L. H. Bailey Hortorium, Cornell University, *Hortus Third*. New York, N.Y.: McMillan Publishing Co.

Ratcliffe, Dell, *Country Shepherd Herb News*, 451 Collier Church Rd., Comer, Georgia, 30629.

Neil Sperry's Complete Guide to Texas Gardening. Dallas, Texas: Taylor Publishing Co.

Welch, William C., and Greg Grant, *The Southern Heirloom Garden*. Dallas, Texas: Taylor Publishing Co.

Westmacott, Richard, *African-American Gardens and Yards in the Rural South*. Knoxville, Tenn.: The University of Tennessee Press.

Wilson, Jim, *Landscaping with Container Plants*. Boston, Mass.: Houghton Mifflin Co.

Wilson, Jim, *Landscaping with Herbs*. Boston, Mass.: Houghton Mifflin Co.

Wilson, Jim, and Guy Sternberg, *Landscaping with Native Trees*. Boston, Mass.: Houghton Mifflin Co. (out of print)

Wilson, Jim, *Landscaping with Wildflowers*. Boston, Mass.: Houghton Mifflin Co.

Wilson, Jim, *The South Carolina Gardener's Guide*. Franklin, Tenn.: Cool Springs Press.

Retail Nurseries Mentioned in the Text

Flower Market, Inc., 4520 Old Kingston Pike, Knoxville, Tennessee 37919

Garden of Eden Nursery and Landscape, 3520 Central Ave., Hot Springs, Arkansas 71913

Indigo Marsh Nursery, a retail garden center in Florence, South Carolina, specializing in native plants and advanced cultivars of heat-resistant species

Lakewood Gardens, 3101 North Hills Blvd., North Little Rock, Arkansas 72116

Plantation Nursery Co., Meridianville, Alabama 35759

Sterling Nurseries, 320 Senate Street, Columbia, South Carolina 29201

Tallahassee Nurseries, Inc., 2911 Thomasville Road, Tallahassee, Florida 32312

The Plant Shoppe, 5416 N.W. 8th Ave., Gainesville, Florida 32605

Dan West Garden Center, 4763 Poplar Ave., Memphis, Tennessee 38117

Zimlich's Patio and Garden Center, 2650 Dauphin St., Mobile, AL 36606

Wholesale Nursery

This corporation does not sell directly to home gardeners, only to retail garden centers.

San Felasco Nurseries, Inc.

Botanical Gardens and University Test Gardens Mentioned in the Text

Callaway Gardens, Pine Mountain, Georgia

Riverbanks Zoo and Botanical Gardens, Columbia, South Carolina

Daniel Stowe Botanical Garden, Belmont, North Carolina

University of Georgia, Department of Horticulture, Athens, Georgia

Oklahoma State University, Oklahoma City Campus, Oklahoma

University of Tennessee, Department of Horticulture, Knoxville, Tennessee

Wholesale Flower Seed and Plant Breeders and Producers

Conservatively speaking, there may be two hundred companies worldwide who specialize in breeding and producing new and established varieties and cultivars of ornamentals. They don't sell directly to home gardeners, but rather to mail-order seed and plant companies and greenhouse producers of bedding plants. I have mentioned a few wholesale companies by name, not to show favoritism, but to acknowledge their involvement in breeding plants that can stand up to high heat and humidity.

Acknowledgments

Many people have helped me by providing photo-ops, information on cultivars for containers, and technical expertise on manufactured soils.

In particular, I am grateful to:

The several garden centers, botanical gardens, and keen amateur gardeners who supplied the reports in chapter 6.

Park Seed Co., Greenwood, SC, for their impeccable trials of all kinds of flowers and their special plantings in containers. Their Flower Festival is held the third week in June each year and is open to the public.

Ball Horticultural, West Chicago, Illinois, for their superb trials of plants in containers and hanging baskets.

Steve Jaharian and Dr. Hugh Poole of Fafard, Inc., Anderson, SC, makers of high-quality manufactured soils for containers. They fact-checked my text on potting soils and feeding plants.

My fellow Master Gardener and technical consultant Robert F. Polomski who, at his office at Clemson University, has access to the latest scientific and technical literature.

Henry Marc Cathey, Ph.D., author of *Heat Zone Gardening*, who verified the hardiness and heat-zone ranges for these plants.

Photo Credits

Most of the photos are by the author, using a Nikon 8008-S with a 28–85 mm zoom lens or a 60 mm Nikor Micro lens. Some of the photos were supplied by William D. (Bill) Adams of Houston, Texas, and Plant Pics, Duluth, Minnesota.

Index

Numbers in *italics* indicate photographs.